Spid

The Rod Thornhill Story

Ian Thornhill

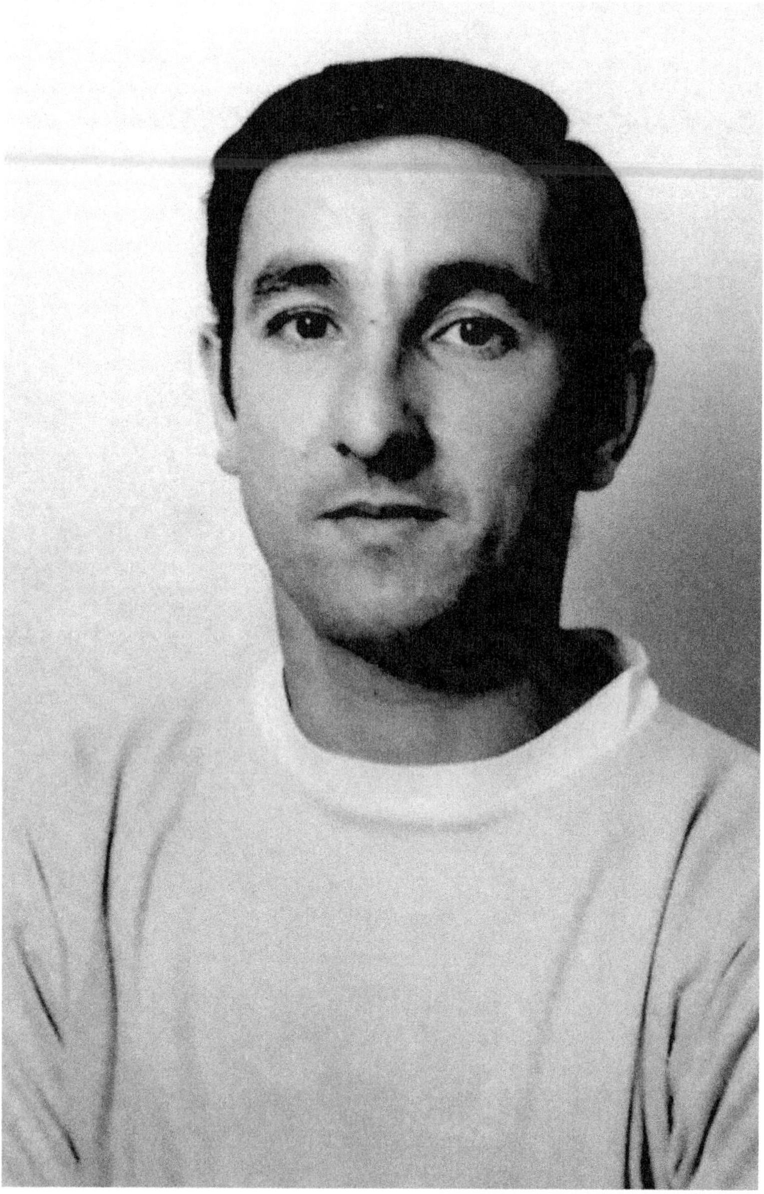

Copyright © 2022

All Rights Reserved

Table of Contents

Dedication i
Acknowledgements ii
About The Author iii
Introduction 1
Chapter 1: Growing Up In Reading 6
Chapter 2: Little Spider 14
Chapter 3: 1960-63: The Amateur Years 22
Chapter 4: 1963-64 – Someone Is Pivoting, Rod Thornhill? Yes! 38
Chapter 5: 1964-65 - Hot Shot Rodney Rocks Watford 56
Chapter 6: 1965-66 – Reading Bank on Thornhill 77
Chapter 7: 1966-67 - Mr. Versatility 100
Chapter 8: 1967-68 - Ace in the Pack 123
Chapter 9: 1968-69 - Mr Reliability 141
Chapter 10: 1969-70 – Injuries and Transfer Lists 164
Chapter 11: 1970-71 – The Dolphins Of Poole 183
Chapter 12 1971-72 – The Final Countdown 199
Chapter 13: Life After Football 209

Dedication

For the Thornhill, Burrell family, and all Reading FC supporters worldwide.

Acknowledgements

There are lots of people who have helped with advice information and assisted with memorabilia, so I would like to express my deepest appreciation and give a warm thank you to the following for their assistance.

David Downs, Roger Titford, Roger Ware, Rachel Walden, Chris Reeves, Chris Lee, Stephen Rex, and of course, Rod and Jan Thornhill.

A very special and particular thank you to my wife, Roxie, for putting up with me whilst I trawled through pages and pages of newspaper reports on the internet! It would not be possible without you.

About The Author

Ian Thornhill is the youngest son of Rodney Thornhill. He is a season ticket holder at Reading FC and was a youth team football coach for 20 years. He once appeared as a contestant on Bargain Hunt. He lives in Shinfield, near Reading with his wife, Roxie, and a mischievous beagle called Bella.

Introduction

Rod Of The Rovers

Who of you remembers Roy of the Rovers? For those who do not, let me explain. Roy Race was a cartoon character who played for Melchester Rovers and had his own comic in the 1970s. He would be the hero of many a storyline scoring late goals in important matches to save the day or win cup finals. You can still hear commentators and football pundits today refer to "Roy of the Rovers" moments when something extraordinary happens in a match.

I loved reading the Roy of the Rovers comics, and whilst writing this book, I became aware of the origins of Roy of the Rovers, a story that started in the Tiger comic in 1954 and continues to this day in a digital guise.

The origins of Roy of the Rovers begin like this: Roy Race is playing for his local youth side, Milston Youth Club, and unbeknown to Roy, a talent spotter from Melchester Rovers is watching the game. The talent spotter approaches Roy and asks him to come to the ground on Saturday to play for the "A" team. Roy is thrilled as he had often dreamed of playing for a club like Melchester Rovers but never considered himself good enough. Of course, Roy would be good enough and would go on to play for the first team and score vital goals in matches to win leagues and cups galore!

As I read the origins of Roy of the Rovers, although not on the grand scale of the made-up Roy Race, there were similarities with Rod's career. Rod was playing for Berkshire County Sports when he was spotted by a scout for his local team, Reading FC, a team he had supported as a boy and had been to watch matches with his dad. Like Roy Race, Rod started off in the "A" Team and progressed through to the reserves and onto his ultimate goal of playing for the first team where he was to score 4 goals in the first 29 minutes of a league match against Watford, a real Roy of the Rovers moment!

As a young boy or girl kicking a ball around in the park or their back gardens, the dream is to play for the team they support, whether it be Manchester Utd, Liverpool or their local professional league club, like Reading, and then to score lots of goals playing in the famous shirt. But for most, it is just a dream.

Rod achieved his dream of playing for his local professional team. He had offers to play for other teams when he was playing, but his heart was always with Reading FC, and he gave it his all. I hope this book goes some way to telling his story through good and bad times playing for Reading in the 1960s.

The following is drawn from Rod's own accounts of his time of growing up, playing football, and life after football, with help from his wife, Janet. The family kept newspaper reports from The Berkshire/Reading Chronicle and Evening Post over the years, and I have used some of the original clippings, so the quality of some of the pictures are not the best, but I wanted to use them as they are an important part of our family growing up.

As well as newspaper clippings, our family also kept all of Rod's programmes he acquired over his playing career, and I have used some of Roy Bentley's programme notes he made commenting on the previous week's games. I have also researched newspaper reports from the Reading Library and the British Newspaper Archive Website covering the dates of Rod's career, and David Downs, a former club historian, has helped with some statistics.

At first, this was just a project to gather together Rod's recollections of his playing career as he is one of many footballers who are now suffering from Alzheimer's Disease after heading the ball so many times throughout his football career, and the family wanted some kind of record of his memories as a keepsake. As time went on and he recounted his time playing, I decided that it would be good to try and write his story as best I could despite having had no experience of writing a book before. This is my effort for what it's worth! I hope you enjoy it as much as I enjoyed researching and writing it!

A few things to remember when reading the book are that things were slightly different in Rod's playing days than they are today, as follows:

- Only 2 points for a win, 1 point for a draw.
- The divisions were simply 1st Division, 2nd Division, 3rd Division, and the 4th Division, so today's Premiership was the equivalent of Division 1.
- In Division 3, only the top 2 went up, and the bottom 4 went down, with 4 teams coming up from Division 4.
- There were no playoffs.
- Teams were not allowed substitutes until one was introduced for the 1965/66 season, which was supposed to be for injuries only.
- Reading were not called the "Royals" in the 1960s. They were nicknamed "The Biscuit Men" as Reading was famous for biscuits back then due to the Huntley and Palmer factories in the town.
- There were no squad numbers, just the 1-12 jersey each week. If you had the number 5 jersey, you knew you would be playing at centre half, and the number 9 jersey was always for the striker. You knew your position from the number on the back of your shirt!
- Rod's nickname of "Spider" came from the local press due to his long gangly frame. Rod says he got the

nickname due to his height, but also, if he were marking you, he would be all over you!

So, get yourself a cup of tea, Rod's favourite tipple, because today's personality is –

★ *TODAY'S PERSONALITY*

Rodney Thornhill

Inside Forward

A local born player who assisted our Club as an amateur player from 20th August, 1960, until he signed as a professional player on 27th May, 1963.

Chapter 1: Growing Up In Reading

A young Rod outside 162 Cressingham Road, Reading

Rodney Derek Thornhill was born during the Second World War on 24th January 1942. He was one of nine children living in a three-bedroom house at 162 Cressingham Road in Whitley, a suburb of Reading in Berkshire.

One of Rod's earliest memories growing up was of a horse and cart that used to come down Cressingham Road to deliver the milk. Cressingham Road was on a steep hill, and the milkman had to put the brake on the cart to stop it from sliding down the hill. When the milkman got to 162, he would put a nose bag on the horse with food in it, whilst the milkman had a cup of tea, and Rod remembers feeding the horse whilst he was outside his house. In later life, Rod would follow in the footsteps of the horse and cartman and become a milkman himself, albeit in an electric-powered milk float rather than a horse-drawn cart!

There were steep steps leading up to 162, and Rod would always be kicking a ball around the steps, and one of the neighbours would always be yelling at him to "clear off." Rod would then concentrate on trying to keep the ball up and not kick the ball against the steps to quietly hone his football skills.

One of the other neighbours was Rod's age, and he had a new leather football as his parents were a bit more well off than some of the other residents, so Rod would call on this neighbour and then call on his friend "Buster." They would go down to the park next to Hartsbourne Road, where they would have a kick around. Rod remembers them as being good players, so this helped him in his development playing football at an early age, and whenever possible, a local unofficial friendly would be arranged between the children of Cressingham Road and Staverton Road for a local derby match at Long Barn Lane Rec.

Rod's father, Ernest Edward Thornhill, worked for the Southern Electric Board for most of his working life on the Vastern Road in Reading, just behind the central train station. He would cycle to work every day to start at 8 am and return at 5 pm. He was a general maintenance/handyman, and Rod remembers him being a well-respected man to whom other workers would go for general advice or help. He could turn his hand to a number of different jobs and was sent out by the SEB to work on anything from electric work, bricklaying or repairing anything that was broken.

Rod remembers, he was a good father, but a stern man and woe betide you if you got caught doing something you shouldn't have been doing! He was a generous man, though, as the Electric Board gave him allotment plots near some of the buildings he maintained. However, he had a big garden at 162, so he would let other people use his plot for free.

Rod's Mum, Nelly, looked after all the kids and had a cleaning job. Every day she would walk up the hill on Cressingham Road and clean for Mr. Barnes, who had a bungalow on the hill, and then she would be off to do some cleaning at Leighton Park School at the end of Cressingham Road. She had several other cleaning jobs, and she would walk to every one of them.

When Rod was older and earning money playing football, he would pick his mum up every Friday to save her legs!

When Rod was about 6 years old, she would regularly send him off to the shop on Cressingham Road to get her whatever she needed. Although it was a big family, Rod's mum would always make sure that all the kids would get Christmas presents with six or seven presents in each of their stockings. However, there were no family holidays, as his Mother and Father couldn't afford a family holiday away. Instead, there were occasional day trips to Southsea by Coach.

Rod was the third youngest in a family of nine. Desmond, who they called Jack, was the eldest and, according to Rod, had the brains of the family, attending a specialist school in Bournemouth. Joan was the next oldest, and Alan was the third oldest. Alan, who worked as a farmer, went on to have seven children himself. Pat, Brian, Daphne and Colin came next in the sibling order, and Rod was the seventh child in the family. His younger siblings were his brother Bob, and Jill was the youngest of the family.

Rod remembers Daphne would sometimes come home late and crawl up the drainpipe to avoid his father, who would always be ready to catch any of his brothers and sisters coming home late or being out when they shouldn't be. If his father had fallen asleep in his chair, his mother would be ready to let them in without his father knowing!

Rod was the only member of the family to be good at sport, although his younger brother Bob would always be kicking a ball around with Rod.

The family only had one bicycle between all of them, and Rod's older brothers, who had motorcycles as they got older, made him a bicycle so he could go to watch football with his father. They got a frame from the local scrapyard and then found some wheels. They also managed to find some straight handlebars, which Rod says was a luxury in those days. Rod painted the bike in blue and white after the colours of Reading FC. He was now able to go with his father to watch Reading FC matches at Elm Park. Rod and his father would cycle to Elm Park during the 1950s to watch as many home games as they could afford, and in particular, they would always go to the Boxing Day match as a tradition.

They would leave their bikes unlocked just outside the ground next to the South Stand, and they would never get stolen. It was not the done thing to steal someone else's bike when they were at a football match in those days. They would then stand in the main stand opposite to where the players came out. Rod was still quite small for his age, and he had trouble seeing the play sometimes, especially in big games, so he would be picked up and put over the wall at the front of the terracing where he would sit next to the pitch and watch the game. A lot of the children would do this, so there would always be a line of children alongside the pitch for big matches; otherwise, he would try to see from the terracing, about 10 rows back from the front where his dad would stand.

Rod remembers his father had some pretty colourful language when he was watching the games and would always be berating the referee! Rod remembers seeing players such as Ronnie Blackman the Centre Forward, Ray Reeves, a big burly full back and the captain of the side, Stan Wicks playing at the back, Dave Meeson was goalkeeper, Bobby Campbell, who ended up as assistant manager, Wally Hinshelwood was left-wing, and Sammy Chung, who went on to manage Wolves in the seventies.

He also remembers seeing Matt Busby's Man Utd playing Reading in an FA Cup Third Round match when Reading took a surprising 1-0 lead through Dennis Uphill and were looking to cause a major upset before Colin Webster scored a late equaliser. Matt Busby said after the game that he had almost given the game up! Reading lost the replay 4-1 in the snow at Old Trafford.

READING: Standing: McLuckie, Neate, Evans, Meeson, Lacey, Reeves. Sitting: Buck Wheeler, Walker, Shreeve, Goodall.

With the football bug really kicking in, Rod ventured up to Wembley with his friend Brian who lived in Shinfield, just outside of Reading. Rod wouldn't have gone on his own, but Brian was a bit more confident than Rod. Without their parent's knowledge, they were going; they got on a train to London to watch England draw 2-2 with Austria on November 28th, 1951, with the likes of Billy Wright, Alf Ramsey and Nat Lofthouse starring for England.

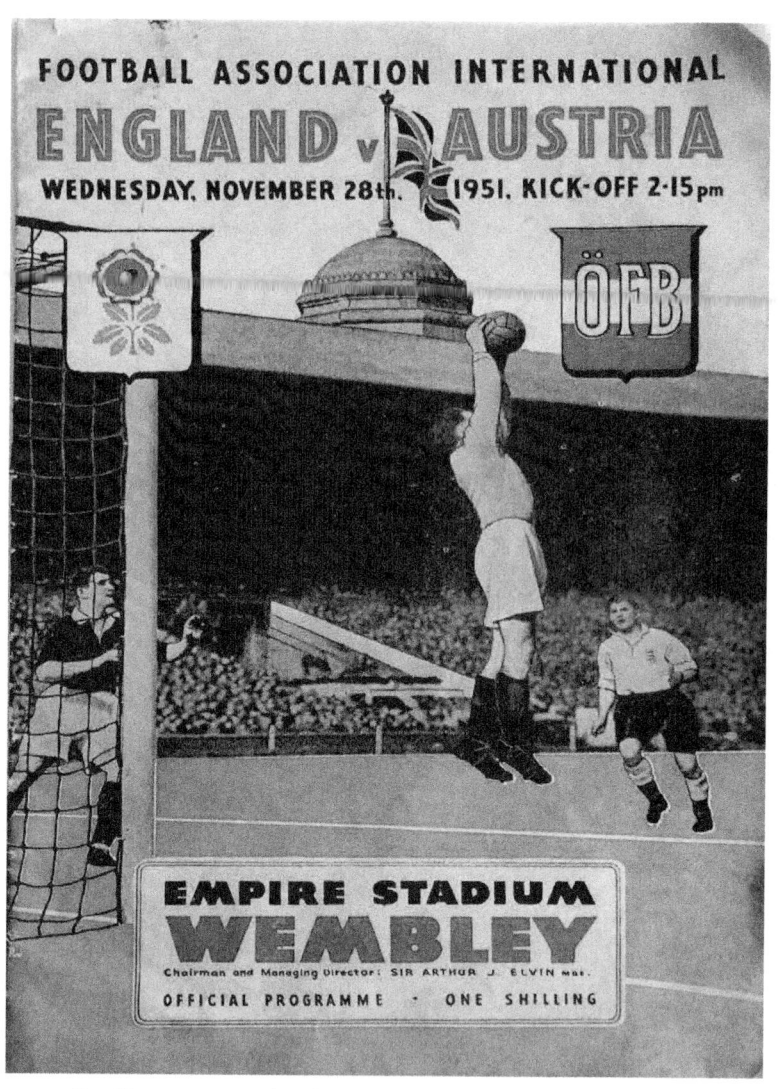

Rod's program he kept of England v Austria 1951

Chapter 2: Little Spider

Ridgeway Primary School Football Team 1952 – Rod is on the back row, far right.

Rod started junior school at Ridgeway School in Whitley and played in the school team against other schools in the area. When he was 11 years old, he left to go to EP Collier School in Reading, close to where his father worked, although Rod would cycle the four-mile journey to school on his own every day.

When Rod started playing football for the schools, they used a leather ball with thick laces to tie the leather together, which was very different from the footballs they use today. They were brown and heavy, and Rod remembers that if you headed the part of the ball with the laces on it or you didn't head it properly, you could catch a part of the lace in your eye, and it would hurt. His football boots were made of leather, and he had to put his own studs in. The studs had three layers of leather and three nails you had to punch through.

There were six studs on the boot, and Rod remembers having to make his own nails as well.

At this time, Rod was showing no signs of the "Spider" nickname he would be given by the local newspapers due to his height and the way he would be all over his marker when he started playing professionally. He wasn't growing much early on, and he was still quite small when he was playing for the school team, but his lack of height wasn't affecting his football. Rod was playing on the left-wing as a nippy winger in his school days, and as he reached the age of 13 to 14, he started to get taller.

One of his friends on the school team was Peter Toft, who played in goal. It was Peter who would attend training with Rod at Elm Park when they got older. Peter later went on to become a well-known local football administrator as well as being the fixture secretary for the local Reading Combination League and Referee's appointment Secretary.

EP Collier School 1954-55 Season – Rod is on the back row on the far right next to his friend, Goalkeeper Peter Toft.

While Rod attended EP Collier School, he was to meet his future wife, Janet Adkins. Rod and Janet were in the same year, although the boys and girls were separated for classes, and Rod remembers them "hooking up" straight away when he joined EP Collier at the age of 11. Rod would escort Janet to the town centre at the end of school, and Janet would catch the trolley bus home to Westwood Road in Tilehurst. Rod would then cycle back home from town.

They were well known to the teachers for their budding relationship, and the teachers would see them walking out of school holding hands and would say hello or make a friendly comment to them as they passed. They were banned from holding hands in school, though. That was definitely not allowed at that time!

Rod's future wife, Janet Adkins, top row, far right. EP Collier School – 1954

When Rod wasn't playing football in school or kicking a ball about with friends, he would be hanging out with Janet. He would cycle 6 miles up to the bungalow in Westwood Road in Tilehurst, where she lived. Her dad had been in the Navy during the Second World War, and he was quite a handyman as he had built the house that they lived in himself.

Rod started staying at Janet's house on Saturday nights when they were only 13 or 14 years old, staying in separate rooms, of course. Rod would then have to cycle back to attend Sunday school the next morning.

There wasn't a lot to do for a young couple in those days, and they would go to the cinema if they could afford it, but that would not be very often. Rod, though, would have his own way of getting into the cinema to watch a film for free!

Rod remembers there being a cinema on Broad Street called The Odeon, and The Pavillion was on the Oxford Road as you went out of the town to the west. Rod, and his friend Butch, would wait at the back of the Odeon until a film had finished in the auditorium and then when they were all coming out of the back door, they would hold the door open for anyone coming out and would sneak in the back door before it closed, so they didn't have to pay.

At the Pavilion through, it was a lot harder as there wasn't a back door, it was a door on the side that led to the street, and they always had someone inside guarding the door. They did manage to get in a couple of times, though and hid in the toilet for half an hour until the film was about to start, and then they would casually walk in as if they had paid!

There was also another cinema near where he lived called The Savoy on the Basingstoke Road in Reading, and they would get in using the same method as the Odeon. They never got caught, so it seems they had perfected this method well!

Before Rod and Janet left school, Janet's French teacher took a class to Switzerland and offered to take Rod and Janet as well. It took quite a few months of newspaper rounds between them before they had saved enough money for the trip. They caught the train to Basel in Switzerland, and when they had been there a few days, they all realised that the teacher had a boyfriend there, which may have been the real reason for the trip!

Whilst they were in Switzerland, they visited the gorgeous town of Interlaken, in the Jungfrau region. In Interlaken, Rod and Janet were engaged at the age of 15 when their friends on the trip arranged to buy Janet an engagement ring.

They both left school at 15 and got jobs in the town centre of Reading. Janet's parents didn't want her to leave school until she was 16, but Janet decided to leave before then and did not tell them. Every morning, her parents thought she was going to school when she was, in fact, going into town to work in a hairdresser. One morning, she walked into Heelas in Broad Street as they were advertising and asked if she could work there, and they offered her a job there and then.

Rod had got a job at Holmes Furnishers in Hosier Street on the main road where the trolleybuses used to go. Here he learnt to be a French Polisher, a trade he was to continue whilst still playing professional football. The houses and businesses in Hosier Street and the surrounding roads were demolished in the 1970s to make way for the Butts Centre Shopping centre.

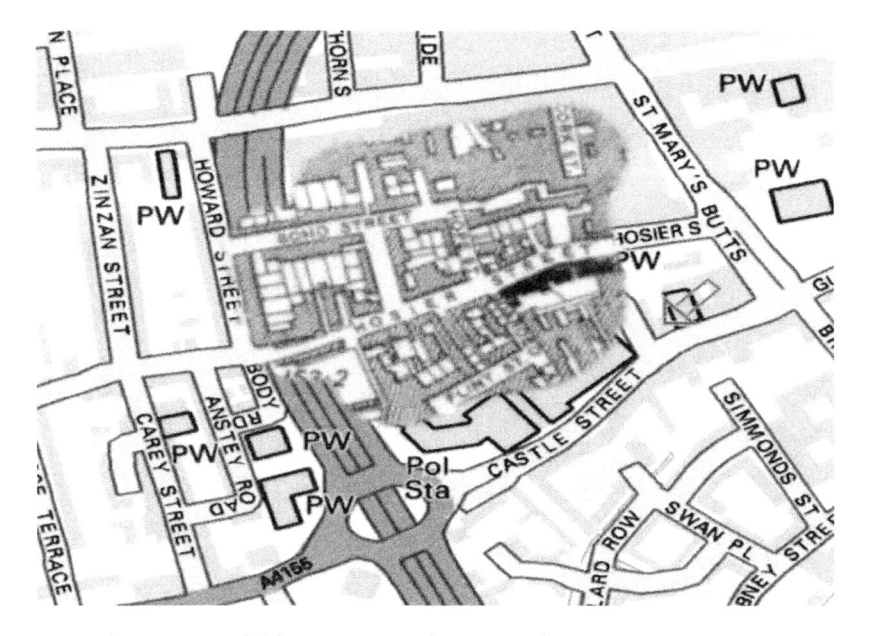

Courtesy of Chris Lee – The map shows Hosier Street where Rod worked at Holmes Furnishing, and the roads demolished to make way for the Butts Centre

Every lunchtime, Rod and Janet would meet in the St Mary's Church in central Reading next to Heelas, where they would have their sandwiches before returning to work.

Janet had an argument with her dad one day, and it was severe enough for her to gather some of her belongings and get on a trolley bus to head to 162 Cressingham Road and ask Rod's mum if she could stay. "No, you cannot," was the reply "we've got far too many in this house as it is!"

Rod and Janet persisted, though, and his mum told her she could share the front living room with Nancy, Brother Brian's girlfriend, so she slept in the armchair for the night before going home the next day. It was looking like it was time for Rod and Janet to try and find a place of their own to live.

Chapter 3: 1960-63: The Amateur Years

Rod & Janet's wedding in 1961

Rod and Janet's local place to hang out in their teenage years was at the Reading YMCA on Parkside Road in Reading, every Tuesday and Thursday evening. Rod would play snooker, table tennis and 5 a side football in the courtyard just outside the YMCA building, and Janet would help out in the café voluntarily.

Rod was now regularly playing in league matches for the YMCA against other local YMCA centres, and he was also playing for Berkshire County Sports against London sides.

It was playing in one match for Berkshire County Sports when Rod remembers the ball going out of play on the left wing where he was playing. Someone who was watching the game from the touchlines retrieved the ball for Rod and passed it back to him. Rod looked and said to him, "I recognise you." before turning his attention back to the match. He was sure it was someone from the football club as it was not unknown for scouts to be on the touchline at local matches looking to unearth any local talent for the club, but Rod didn't think anything of it.

It was towards the end of March in 1960, while Rod was training with the other players in the team in the courtyard at the YMCA, Mr. Briggs, his YMCA football manager, came out of the building and said, "Rod, get on your bike and go down to the football club now." Rod was a bit confused and asked why. "Harry Johnstone wants to talk to you." Harry Johnstone was the Reading FC manager at that time, so Rod got on his bike and rode as fast as he could to the football stadium. It was a mere two-minute bike ride from the YMCA to the football ground. Rod had no idea that the club was interested in him until this time, but he now had a good feeling.

Rod met Harry Johnstone at the ground, who told him that he wanted to sign him there and then, and he wanted him to play for the 'A' team on a Saturday. At that time, the 'A' team was just below the reserve side and consisted of mostly youth players, but it was an excellent platform to make your way to the first team if you could impress week in, week out. Rod was overjoyed and didn't need to think about it or discuss it with anyone. He signed the amateur forms straight away! It was then Rod realised who the man was who had passed the ball back to him the time he was playing for the YMCA; it was Bobby Campbell, Harry Johnstone's assistant.

Rod rode back to the YMCA to tell Mr. Briggs, who already had a smile on his face when he arrived! Rod rode back to tell his parents as quickly as he could. His dad was sitting in his usual chair in the kitchen and shouted at Rod, "Why are you rushing around, Lad?" Rod told him that he had just signed for Reading. His dad didn't believe him at first. They knew he had been playing for Reading Schools and Berkshire County Sports, but they were still surprised and overjoyed when Rod told them the good news.

As soon as he could, Rod went out to purchase a new pair of football boots for just under £2 from Blakes Sport Shop in Minster Street in Reading. Rod remembers buying all his football gear from this sports shop which survived in Reading for many years.

The only drawback for signing amateur forms for Reading was that he was no longer able to play for the YMCA, but the excitement of playing for Reading and the fact his friend from EP Collier (and YMCA) Peter Toft, was able to come along training at Elm Park as well, certainly made up for the disappointment.

At first, there would be training on Tuesday and Thursday evenings, and they would be quite brutal if they didn't think you were up to it as they would just let you go without any warning, but he continued to train with them and then play in 'A' team matches in the local leagues on a Saturday.

Rod started playing for the 'A' team at left half back. This was when most teams were still using the "WM" formation perfected by the Arsenal manager Herbert Chapman in the mid-1920s. An example of the formation can be seen below in a match from Rod's first season as a professional against Colchester United in 1963.

always FARM FRESH from BAYLIS supermarkets
Broad St. & Erleigh Rd. Reading · Caversham · Newbury · Abingdon

Reading
Shirts: Blue and White Hoops
Knickers: White

RIGHT

2
Arthur Wilkie
1

LEFT

Johnnie Walker
3
Gordon Neate

4
Maurice Evans
5
Dick Spiers
6
Rodney Thornhill

7
Jimmy Wheeler
Peter Kerr
8
9
Jimmy Martin
Denis Allen
10
11
Freddie Jones

REFEREE:
Mr. N. C. H. Burtenshaw
(Great Yarmouth)

HIGGS — WINES SPIRITS BEERS — DELIVERED TO YOUR HOME — TEL READING 53681

LINESMEN:
RED FLAG
Mr. D. R. G. Nippard
(Bournemouth)

YELLOW FLAG
Mr. L. Newsom
(London)

Wright
11
10
Stark
King
9
8
Hunt
Grice
7

Docherty
6
Rutter
5
McCrohan
4

Fowler
3
1
Ramage
Woods
2

LEFT

RIGHT

Colchester Utd.

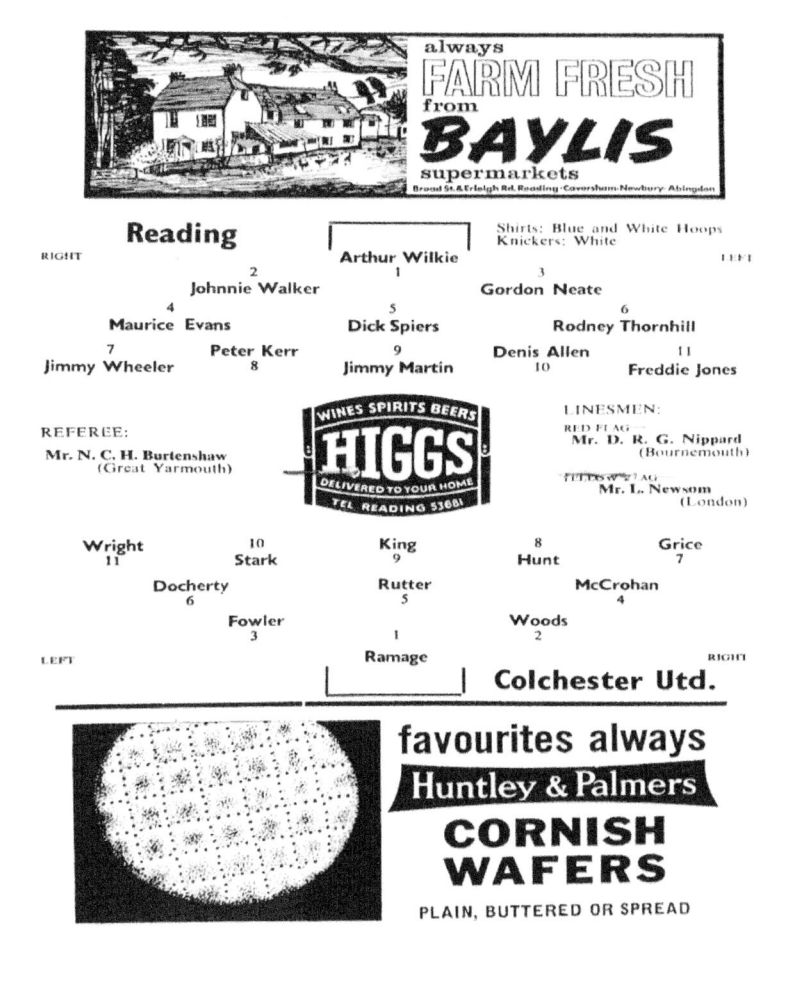

favourites always Huntley & Palmers CORNISH WAFERS
PLAIN, BUTTERED OR SPREAD

The 'A' team would play in the Hampshire League in Division 1 on a Saturday with opposition from the Hampshire area, and it also included other professional clubs, such as Southampton, Portsmouth and Bournemouth, who would also run an 'A' side to help with the development of the younger players.

On 23rd September 1960, with both the first team and reserve team playing away, the 'A' team got the chance to play at Elm Park, and this was Rod's first taste of playing football on the hallowed turf where he had watched the first team from the stands. The 'A' team rose to the occasion and thrashed Christchurch 12-0!

On 17th December 1960, Rod scored his first goal for the 'A' team in a 1-1 draw against Andover, with the Reading team praised for playing good football. In the return match at home, Reading would lose 3-1 but would again be praised by the local press for *'playing attractive football played the correct way.'*

Whilst playing for the 'A' team in a match against Totton AFC on 4th March 1961, the ball was played back to Rod at the kick-off by Reading Captain Rose, who carried on upfield. Rod was able to pick out a pass to Rose, who scored in less than 10 seconds from the start of the game. Unfortunately, they went on to lose the game 3-2. Rod remembers the team would always finish mid-table and often win one week and then lose the next.

His first season as an amateur would be playing for the 'A' team only, with Rod hoping he would be kept on for the following season.

Hampshire League Division 1 League Table 1960-61

	Team	PL	W	D	L	F	A	Pts
1	Salisbury Town	30	22	5	3	80	32	49
2	Fareham Town	30	21	4	5	86	37	46
3	Andover	30	18	8	4	98	37	44
4	Newport (IOW)	30	18	6	6	83	53	40
5	Portsmouth 'A'	30	13	6	11	59	42	31
6	Alton Town	30	12	6	12	62	52	30
7	Waterlooville	30	11	7	12	62	46	29
8	Basingstoke	30	11	5	14	68	61	27
9	Southampton 'A'	30	11	5	14	52	49	27
10	**Reading 'A'**	**30**	**11**	**5**	**14**	**56**	**58**	**27**
11	Bournemouth 'A'	30	11	5	14	51	53	27
12	Gosport Borough	30	11	3	16	73	73	25
13	Cowes	30	10	5	15	55	71	25
14	Notley Sports	30	9	7	14	45	65	25
15	Totton AFC (R)	30	7	4	19	36	87	18
16	Christchurch (R)	30	2	1	27	33	171	5

Rod's 1961-62 season started well as he continued to play for the 'A' team and impress the coaching staff. A report of the match against Portsmouth, in a 2-0 win, described Rod's performance as outstanding. Two weeks later, Rod made his debut at the right half position for the reserves in an away match to Birmingham City Reserves on 4th October 1961.

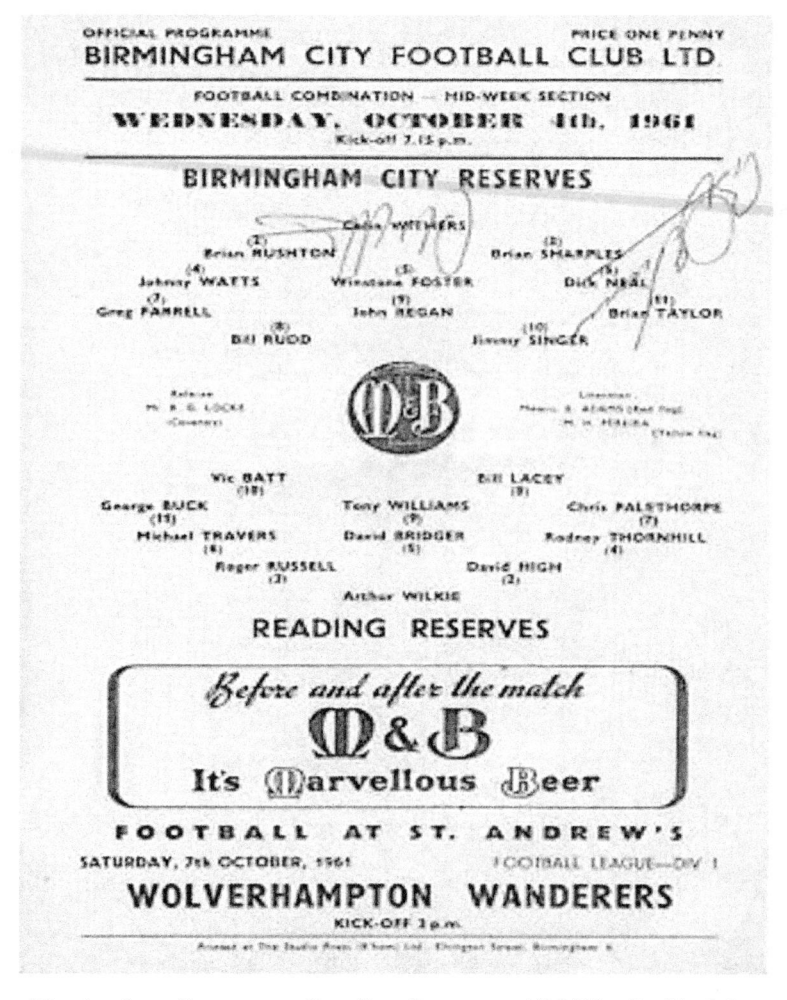

Birmingham Reserves v Reading Reserves 4/10/61 – Rod's debut for Reading Reserves

During the season, Rod was getting more and more matches in the reserves, who would play on a Wednesday in the Combination League against teams in the southern half of the country and top London-based League clubs. This was a chance to rub shoulders with some of the first team professionals and play against some first-team players from other clubs who were either returning from injury or who had fallen out of favour in the first team.

The season continued for Rod playing in all matches for the 'A' team whilst occasionally playing for the reserves. Rod was now on his way to his Spider status at just over 6 feet, and his height meant that he now switched to playing in the backline for the reserves and Rod's versatility was showing early on in his career, being able to play on the left or right side.

The "A" team continued to hover around the middle of the table during this season, losing one more game than they won and finishing 8th at the end of the season. By coincidence, the reserves finished in 8th place, but this time winning four more than they lost.

Hampshire League Division 1 League Table 1961-62

	Team	PL	W	D	L	F	A	Pts
1	Andover	30	19	4	7	83	39	42
2	Salisbury Town	30	17	5	8	72	52	39
3	Gosport Borough	30	16	7	7	58	45	39
4	Alton Town	30	15	6	9	66	51	36
5	Portsmouth 'A'	30	15	6	19	68	48	36
6	Fareham Town	30	15	3	12	54	45	33
7	Cowes	30	13	4	13	44	60	30
8	**Reading 'A'**	**30**	**14**	**1**	**15**	**67**	**59**	**29**
9	Basingstoke	30	12	5	13	71	62	29
10	Waterlooville	30	12	5	13	57	60	29
11	Bournemouth 'A'	30	11	5	14	49	55	27
12	Netley Sports	30	11	3	16	48	71	25
13	Newport (IOW)	30	9	6	15	60	76	24
14	Southampton 'A'	30	9	5	16	53	62	23
15	Thorneycroft (R)	30	9	3	18	54	84	21
16	Swaythling (R)	30	7	2	21	38	80	16

Combination League Division 2 League Table 1961-62

	Team	PL	W	D	L	F	A	Pts
1	Orient Reserves	34	21	6	7	74	42	48
2	Portsmouth Reserves	34	20	6	8	72	47	46
3	Birmingham City Reserve	34	19	7	8	58	45	45
4	Watford Reserves	34	18	4	12	76	55	40
5	Chelsea Reserves	34	17	5	12	84	59	39
6	Millwall Reserves	34	15	9	10	86	64	39
7	Bournemouth Reserves	34	16	6	12	65	50	38
8	**Reading Reserves**	34	**16**	**6**	**12**	**62**	**50**	**38**
9	Swindon Reserves	34	13	8	13	58	58	34
10	Southend Utd Reserves	34	15	4	15	63	73	34
11	Coventry City Reserves	34	13	7	14	66	62	33
12	Southampton Reserves	34	13	6	15	68	62	32
13	Fulham Reserves	34	12	7	15	55	72	31
14	Aldershot Reserves	34	10	9	15	48	63	29
15	Charlton Reserves	34	10	6	18	52	74	26
16	Brighton Reserves	34	7	8	19	42	77	22
17	Brentford Reserves	34	6	9	19	36	73	21
18	QPR Reserves	34	6	5	23	41	90	17

Rod was still working for Holmes Furnishings as an apprentice when he signed for Reading. Holmes Furnishings had a shop front on St Mary Butts in Reading with a workshop in Hosier Street. The ground floor was the carpet department, and Rod and his boss Ray Field worked on the first floor with the Upholstery workshop on the second floor.

Playing and training for the 'A-Team' didn't have an impact for Rod on his work at Holmes as the training was in the evening and matches were on a Saturday afternoon, but as Rod progressed into the reserves, he had to take time off for occasional training and travelling to matches on a Wednesday, so Rod had to have a word with the manager of Holmes, Mr. Raymont.

He had spoken to Ray, his immediate boss, to say that he needed to speak to Mr. Raymont about taking some time off for his football. Rod told him that he was playing football for Reading, and Mr. Raymont replied by saying, "I know." Rod carried on and said to him that he might need to take time off on a Wednesday to travel to and play reserves matches, mostly in the London area, but sometimes as far away as Coventry. Mr. Raymont told him, "That's fine, don't worry, if you need to take time off, that's all okay."

The next home match that Rod attended, he saw Mr. Raymont and one of the salesmen at Holmes in one of the boxes at Elm Park. It turned out he was a Reading FC supporter and a season ticket holder!

Rod was pretty much able to come and go when he liked in respect of playing football whilst he was working at Holmes. After a while, when his apprenticeship at Holmes had finished, Rod had been getting to know people in the furniture business for French polishing jobs, so he started working for himself from the age of 20 onwards.

At the age of 19, a year after Rod had signed amateur forms for Reading, Rod and Janet were married on 15th April 1961 at St Micheals church in Tilehurst and whilst looking for a place to live, they were fortunate that a friend found them a flat to rent on the King's Road in Reading over Lombard Bank, opposite Reading College.

A year later, their first child, Stephen, was born on 1st September 1962, and it was around this time that they moved back with Janet's mum and dad in Tilehurst as it wasn't working out living above the bank. Janet didn't feel comfortable staying there on her own whilst Rod was playing, particularly on away matches where he would sometimes arrive home late. Living above a bank meant the police often shone their torches into the flat when they reported suspicious activities!

This would only be for 8 months until they could buy a maisonette in Taff Way in Tilehurst, close to the football ground.

The 1962/63 season saw Rod training with the first team and reserves, and he was now one of the first names on the reserve team sheet playing in most matches; a much better season for the reserves saw them finish fifth and the highest scorers in the league.

Rod would also bring Janet along to matches, and she would become friends with Denis Allen's wife, who would bring along her young son, Martin Allen. Martin Allen would go on to have a football career as a player for QPR, West Ham and Portsmouth, as well as being an assistant manager at Reading in 2002. Janet remembers her son, Stephen and Martin kicking a ball about on the pitch at Elm Park.

When Janet wasn't watching with the other wives, she would accompany Rod's dad and then have to listen to him swearing at the referee for most of the match!

Janet remembers Rod was superstitious when he played, and if they won, he would have to wear the same clothes to the next match down to underwear and socks, and she remembers he would always have a bowl of cornflakes when he got home from evening kickoffs.

The big freeze of 1963 saw football postponed all over the country, with temperatures plummeting from the middle of December to February and snow covering the country throughout most of this period. The first team would not play for a further 7 weeks, but the reserve team managed to play one game against Brentford during this period at Griffin Park on a rock-hard pitch covered with a mixture of snow, slush, water and sand! The reserves lost 3-0, with Rod, Mick Travers and Peter Shreeves all sustaining injuries due to the conditions.

Reserve matches resumed at the end of February, but without a first-team manager, as the board had come to a mutual agreement with Harry Johnstone to part company.

The Board appointed ex England and Chelsea Centre Forward Roy Bentley, who was tasked with saving the first team from relegation.

It was a good appointment for Rod as he had marked Roy Bentley a few times during reserve matches. Considering he was up against an ex-England International, Rod had always felt he had done well against him, and he hoped Roy Bentley would remember that.

The first team survived, but only on goal difference at the end of the season and with the reserves finishing bottom of the Combination league, Roy Bentley was looking to re-organise the team in all areas. He must have been impressed with Rod's performances for the reserves, as Rod was offered a professional contract at the end of the season, signing professional forms on 27th May 1963.

Combination League Division 2 League Table 1962-63

	Team	PL	W	D	L	F	A	Pts
1	Chelsea Reserves	34	19	10	5	67	34	48
2	Birmingham City Reserve	34	18	7	9	79	39	43
3	Millwall Reserves	34	18	7	9	79	45	43
4	Brighton Reserves	34	18	4	12	53	53	40
5	Swindon Reserves	34	16	7	11	78	62	39
6	Southampton Reserves	34	15	9	10	63	51	39
7	Coventry City Reserves	34	13	10	11	57	52	36
8	Watford Reserves	34	13	9	12	72	67	35
9	Bournemouth Reserves	34	13	9	12	54	58	35
10	Orient Reserves	34	14	5	15	76	68	33
11	Portsmouth Reserves	34	14	5	15	71	65	33
12	Fulham Reserves	34	12	6	16	50	67	30
13	Brentford Reserves	34	11	7	16	59	71	29
14	Southend Utd Reserves	34	11	5	18	75	90	27
15	Aldershot Reserves	34	11	5	18	48	72	27
16	Charlton Reserves	34	13	1	20	64	97	27
17	QPR Reserves	34	10	5	19	51	76	25
18	**Reading Reserves**	**34**	**7**	**9**	**18**	**54**	**84**	**23**

Chapter 4: 1963-64 – Someone Is Pivoting, Rod Thornhill? Yes!

Reading FC Team Photo 1963-64 – Rod on the back row, third from right.

One of Rod's earliest memories of Roy Bentley's training sessions was when Roy took one of the first training sessions with the team when he joined. Roy told the players that they were just going to go for a nice gentle walk around the streets of Reading, near to the football club. The players thought this would be a nice easy training session for them, but twenty minutes into the walk, Roy told them to start jogging and then it gradually built up to making short sprints in the road and outside people's houses!

Rod remembers that the captain at the time, Johnnie Walker, would always be one of the last to arrive back after any running! With a rigorous pre-season training behind them, pounding the streets of Reading, Roy Bentley looked to give all the players a fresh start in the squad, but he had four key players missing for the first game of the season away to Millwall. David Grant (neck operation), Arthur Wilkie (Elbow injury), Ron Tindall (still playing cricket for Surrey) and Freddie Jones, a new signing from Grimsby (thigh muscle injury), were all ruled out.

Rod was given his first-team debut for the opening match of the season after an impressive display in a 3-1 friendly win against Oxford Utd a few days earlier. In fact, the whole team that played in the friendly match were picked for the game. It was a disappointing start with a 2-0 defeat at Millwall, but Rod, wearing the number 6 jersey, settled in the left-half position well for his debut. Rod doesn't remember his debut very well, but he does remember that "The Den" Millwall's ground was always noisy, intimidating away ground to visit with the home supporters always giving you a hard time.

Still searching for the first win of the season after three games, they travelled to Coventry City, who had scored 11 goals and only conceded 1 from their first 4 games. In front of the biggest crowd they would play in front of for the whole season, Rod retained the number 6 jersey with the team holding the much-fancied Coventry to a 0-0 draw, even getting the ball in the Coventry net twice and both times having the goal ruled out by an offside and an infringement. Roy Bentley described the match as a *"first-class exhibition of football with each and every player giving his best throughout a hard and well-fought game."*

After a 4-1 defeat by Crystal Palace caused by defensive errors, the first win of the season came at home against Mansfield on the 14th September 1963, with Rod scoring his first-ever goal for the club in a thrilling 4-3 win. Reading were 2-0 up after 10 minutes of the game, and 4 minutes later, Rod raced onto an Alan Morris cross-field pass to fire in an unstoppable shot from 30 yards out to make it 3-0. Mansfield staged an incredible comeback and scored 3 goals to level the match before Jimmy Wheeler scored the winner for Reading in the 83rd minute.

A regular feature in the Reading Chronicle was Ron Fennell's cartoons on certain games. He was known by his pen name of "Areff," and overleaf is the report on the Reading v Mansfield match.

It was bad news in the Football League cup though, after a 1-1 home draw with Brentford, they were beaten 2-0 in the replay on 23rd September 1963.

Rod "Spider" Thornhill, far right of the picture, provides cover for Mike Dixon, who punches the ball away against Brentford in the 2-0 cup replay defeat on 23/9/63.

On the terraces, there was unrest with some supporters voicing their concerns that Roy Bentley was not picking Johnnie Petts to play, with chants of *"We want Petts"* and demonstrations outside the ground after one match. Petts, a scheming left half, had been signed from Arsenal before Roy Bentley arrived at the club, and Bentley was favouring Rod in the left half position over Petts. Rod remembers that he did not seem to suit Bentley's style as Petts was a small tricky player, and Bentley was looking for a bigger player who was good in the air and could join the attack quickly. In the press, Roy Bentley was quoted as *"sick of the whole affair."* He told the Reading Chronicle, *"The fans are being* unfair to Petts and to young Thornhill, who is playing so well. I admit he lacks the distribution of Petts, but he is a very hard-working, strong tackling, and efficient defender, and that is what we need."

Rod commented on the situation at the time to the Reading Chronicle by saying, "*I thought I was playing quite well on Saturday, but when the crowd began shouting for Johnny in the second half, it did upset me a bit. I tried not to let it spoil my game, and I hope I'll soon be able to prove to them that I am worth my place in the team.*"

Four games later, however, after Rod had scored against Mansfield, he would discover the roller-coaster emotions of being a professional footballer by being dropped from the first team with Bentley making wholesale changes after only one win in eight games and the team sitting fifth from bottom. "Defensive errors" were again cited due to the team's results, and something Bentley remarked should be *"rectified at all costs."*

New signing Ron Tindall, Mike Dixon, Dennis Allan, Douggie Webb were all dropped along with Rod. Rod went back to playing for the reserves in the Combination League until he got the recall for the first team.

The basic weekly wage Rod was receiving at this time was 11 Pounds, 13 Shillings and 8 pence, which in today's money would be approximately £205. However, bonuses were also paid for winning and getting through cup rounds, so this could boost your weekly wage, with Rod receiving 36 pounds, 1 Shilling and 8 pence in one particularly good week, the equivalent to approximately £630.

Rod was also discovering the perks of becoming a professional footballer. With all professionals paying a subscription to the PFA, they, in turn, received a booklet giving them discounts on a whole variety of things to help a newly married couple!

Having started his first-ever game for the first team away to Millwall, it was ironic for Rod to come back into the team after a 16-game absence against Millwall at home on 14th December 1963. This time, Reading would gain revenge on Millwall with a 1-0 win.

The following match would be against Luton, but Rod would be discovering another perk to becoming a professional footballer, the occasional game of golf, which he was enjoying just prior to the Luton game. However, he does admit to never getting any good at it!

Playing golf at Streatley on a Wednesday Morning before the Luton match.

Douggie Webb is driving off, with Alan Morris, David Bridger, Gordon Neate and Rod on the right.

Reading were sitting in 6th place before the Luton game with Luton third from bottom, so confidence was high of potentially moving up to third place in the table. However, on a hard frozen pitch at Kenilworth Road, they went 2-0 down, and after getting one back, they pressed for an equaliser which never came.

A few games later, on 11th January 1964, Coventry City came, riding high at the top of the league and unbeaten for 12 games. Reading were still in 6th place and looking to challenge for promotion.

A mystery stomach bug struck the Coventry team on the way to Elm Park with Coventry manager Jimmy Hill, forced into a defensive reshuffle just prior to kick off after 4 players went down with the bug. With only 45 minutes to go to kick-off, Hill replaced left half, Farmer, with a youngster named Bruck, only to find out Bruck was in a worse state than Farmer and he was then replaced with John Sillett, who had only come along for the ride as he was still recovering from a cracked kneecap!

In front of the highest attendance of the season at Elm Park, 17,102 including 4,000 noisy Coventry fans, the supporters saw Reading ex-player, Jimmy Whitehouse, pop up unmarked in the Reading area in the first half to score twice past the Reading keeper, Arthur Wilkie, in the space of 60 seconds after 17 minutes.

As the second half started, Coventry appeared to be coasting at 2-0, but Reading were not giving in just yet and were fighting for every ball and putting City on the back foot.

After 76 minutes, the referee awarded Reading an indirect free kick inside the area following an obstruction on centre forward Ron Tindall. Johhny Walker side tapped the free-kick to Peter Kerr, who hammered it into the net to make it 2-1. Then with just 5 minutes to go, Rod popped up in a melee in the Coventry penalty area to grab an important goal to make it 2-2. Reading were unlucky not to win in the final seconds of the game with Rod heading just over the bar from a corner.

Rod commented to the Reading Chronicle after the game, *"Curtis stuck out his foot, trying to get to Denis Allen's long ball down the field. He missed, I swung my left foot at it, and the score was 2-2."*

A report in the national newspaper, The People, the following day contained a short report of the game with the headline *"**THORNHILL IS THE HERO FOR READING.**"*

But perhaps the result was never in much doubt after going 2-0 down as The Coventry Evening Telegraph reported on Reading as their 55-year-old Bogey team having not beaten them for this long, with a headline that read, *"That Old Bogey Remains."* Coventry remained top, with Reading still in sixth place, only three points off third place and with a game in hand.

Areffs report on Reading v Watford with Rod 'pivoting' for the equaliser

A 2-1 defeat at Mansfield followed with Roy Bentley blaming a frost-bound pitch for *'not being conducive for good football with the players finding it difficult to maintain a foothold and control the ball'*. The team slipped to 7th place but still only 4 points off 2nd place in the table, which was the second promotion spot.

Warming up for the Watford match at Elm Park – Rod, Colin Meldrum, Maurice Evans, Dick Spiers, Douggie Webb, Jim Martin and Freddie Jones.

The above photo shows the players gently jogging around Elm Park, and this is something the players would do the Friday before the game on Saturday. Rod says that he would arrive at the ground on a Friday morning and then look at the team list, which Roy Bentley would pin to the notice board to see if he was in the team. If they were in the team, the players would do some light jogging, short sprints and some running up the terraces but nothing too strenuous.

The next game saw them up against Watford, one of their promotion rivals. The match did not start well for Reading as after only 12 minutes of the game, centre forward Jimmy Martin collided with Watford keeper Pat Jennings, and as a result, he had to go off to get treatment for an injury to the right knee.

Substitutes were not allowed until the 1965/66 season, so Reading had to struggle on with 10 men until a heavily strapped up Martin emerged in the second half to play on the left-wing, although he could only kick the ball with his left foot and only then when it was placed in front of him! The grit and determination of the Reading team shone through with three Reading corners forced immediately after Martin's injury.

The first goal came after goalkeeper Arthur Wilkie was fouled in the Reading area. Maurice Evans stepped up and booted the ball upfield for Dennis Allen to fire in the first goal. Reading kept up the pressure in the second half and were rewarded with a second goal after a Douggie Webb miskick hit a Watford defender's foot and went in.

Roy Bentley applauded the players after the match stating in the Chronicle, *"The lads gave us a wonderful display, and it was 100 per cent from the start. What more can I say except that I am delighted with the way they fought for every ball. There is no substitute for sheer hard work in the long run. Wonderful."*

The Reading Chronicle was headlined with "Magnificent Reading" and gave all the players 10 out 10. Once again, Rod was going to experience the highs and lows of professional football, when, after receiving a 10 rating in the Watford game, just a game later, he was dropped back to the reserves with the first team sitting sixth in the table and for Rod, this was the last game he would play for the first team for the rest of season. He would spend the remainder of the season playing for the reserves in the Combination League.

The first team finished 6th in the league at the end of the season, and it would have been interesting to know what would have happened if the playoffs were running at the time, as the team finished off the season strongly with a 5-2 and 4-2 win. However, at that time, it was a simple case of the top two go up, so Reading were resigned once again to another season in Division 3. It was, though, the highest they had finished for 5 seasons and a good turn around since Roy Bentley had joined as manager, having only just avoided relegation the season before.

Rod would go on to have a good relationship with Roy Bentley on and off the field whilst he was the manager. Roy got to know Rod worked as French polisher and would often come over to Rod while they were on their way to an away match on the coach and he would ask Rod's opinion on furniture related matters.

Rod thought he was a good manager with good ideas, but if you didn't do what he had told you, he would have a go at the players. He would always have his tracksuit on in training and would always be joining in, and if there was a first eleven v reserves match, he would always play.

As a first season professional, Rod had played 16 league games for the first team in the left half, scoring 2 goals and with 2 appearances in the League cup. Not a bad season to start your professional career

1963-64 Division 3 Table

	Team	Pl	W	D	L	F	A	Pts
1	Coventry City (P)	46	22	16	8	98	61	60
2	Crystal Palace (P)	46	23	14	9	73	51	60
3	Watford	46	23	12	11	79	59	58
4	Bournemouth	46	24	8	14	79	58	56
5	Bristol City	46	20	15	11	84	64	55
6	**READING**	**46**	**21**	**10**	**15**	**79**	**62**	**52**
7	Mansfield Town	46	20	11	15	76	62	51
8	Hull City	46	16	17	13	73	68	49
9	Oldham Athletic	46	20	8	18	73	70	48
10	Peterborough Utd	46	18	11	17	75	70	47
11	Shrewsbury Town	46	18	11	17	73	80	47
12	Bristol Rovers	46	19	8	19	91	79	46
13	Port Vale	46	16	14	16	53	49	46
14	Southend Utd	46	15	15	16	77	78	45
15	QPR	46	18	9	19	76	78	45
16	Brentford	46	15	14	17	87	80	44
17	Colchester Utd	46	12	19	15	70	68	43
18	Luton Town	46	16	10	20	64	80	42
19	Walsall	46	13	14	19	59	76	40
20	Barnsley	46	12	15	19	68	94	39
21	Millwall (R)	46	14	10	22	53	67	38
22	Crewe Alexandra (R)	46	11	12	23	50	77	34
23	Wrexham (R)	46	13	6	27	75	107	32
24	Notts County (R)	46	9	9	28	45	92	27

1963-64 Combination Division 2 Table

	Team	PL	W	D	L	F	A	Pts
1	Chelsea Reserves	34	21	6	7	74	27	48
2	Portsmouth Reserves	34	20	6	8	79	46	46
3	Fulham Reserves	34	17	9	8	68	52	43
4	Charlton Reserves	34	18	6	10	70	45	42
5	**READING RESERVES**	**34**	**16**	**8**	**10**	**84**	**67**	**40**
6	Swindon Town Reserves	34	16	7	11	80	65	39
7	Birmingham Reserves	34	16	6	12	73	58	38
8	Coventry Reserves	34	14	9	11	66	63	37
9	Millwall Reserves	34	14	9	11	50	54	37
10	Watford Reserves	34	14	8	12	68	60	36
11	Southampton Reserves	34	16	4	14	72	66	36
12	Bournemouth Reserves	34	13	7	14	50	52	33
13	Leyton Orient Reserves	34	11	6	17	58	75	28
14	Brentford Reserves	34	10	7	17	44	74	27
15	Brighton Reserves	34	8	8	18	52	88	24
16	QPR Reserves	34	10	2	22	49	73	22
17	Southend Reserves	34	7	6	21	65	96	20
18	Aldershot Reserves	34	4	8	22	44	85	16

SEASON
1963-4

READING

FOOTBALL CLUB
OFFICIAL PROGRAMME 4d

Chapter 5: 1964-65 - Hot Shot Rodney Rocks Watford

Reading F.C. 1964-65
Directors, Officials and Players

Back Row (lt. to rt.) M. Travers P. Shreeves C. Meldrum D. Bridger M. Dixon R. Thornhill A. Wilkie G. Neate P. Kerr R. Spiers
Centre Row (lt. to rt.) J. Wallbanks (trainer) Barry Rusher Brian Rusher M. Evans J. Petts B. Faulkes J. Walker D. Webb J. Wheeler R. Norton M. Fairchild D. Grant W. Lacey (assistant trainer)
Front Row (lt. to rt.) Mr. F. May (secretary/manager) Mr. W. T. D. Vincent (director) Mr. J. S. Windebank (director) Mr. A. E. Smith (chairman) Mr. F. V. Waller (vice-chairman) Mr. D. P. Baylis (director) Mr. R. Bentley (team manager)
Seated (lt. to rt.) I. Maidment M. Porter B. Knight

Reading FC Team photo 1964/65

After being left out of the first team at the end of the 1963/64 season, Rod was working hard in training to get back into the first team, but he still found himself on the sidelines for the first 4 games of the season.

After a poor display in the third game of the season, losing 2-0 to Southend Utd, Roy Bentley gave his team one more chance before he considered changing the team, but after a 4-0 drubbing away to Shrewsbury in the next game,

Bentley was looking to make sweeping changes for the visit to Barnsley.

Out of the team went Johnny Walker, Mike Fairchild, Peter Shreeves, David Grant and Pat Terry. In came Gordon Neate, Jimmy Wheeler, Denis Allen, Douggie Webb, Peter Kerr and Rod. The surprise selection was Rod coming into the team, not in his usual left half position, but this time as an inside right, a more attacking position. Roy Bentley explained his decision in the Reading Chronicle, *"Rod is in good form this season, and it is on the strength of his flair for quick bursts through the middle that he has been selected."*

The game didn't start well with Jimmy Wheeler going off early on with a hairline fracture after 20 minutes, but the 10 men of Reading were battling well, and went into the half time break at 0-0. A minute after the break, Rod justified his inclusion with a shot that took a deflection off a Barnsley defender and went in to put Reading 1-0 up.

Unfortunately, they could not prevent Barnsley from scoring an equaliser, but it was a hard-fought point, earning praise from the Reading manager as *"a splendid performance."*

Rod in action against Barnsley on 4/9/64

The month of September 1964 would go on to be undoubtedly the best month in Rod's career.

After a 1-0 away win against QPR on 7th September, Reading had a home match on 12th September against newly relegated from Division 2, Scunthorpe, and the match started well for Reading who went into a 1-0 lead when Pat Terry flicked the ball to Rod who headed in the first goal after 35 minutes.

In the second half, the Referee, Mr Rex Spittle, awarded a penalty to Scunthorpe in the 70th minute for handball by Petts after a goalmouth scramble, when it appeared the ball struck his chest. The players surrounded the referee, who consulted the lineman before changing his mind and giving a drop ball. Reading then raced to the other end with Pat Terry crossing beautifully for Rod to run through and score his second to settle the match.

The referee was again involved in controversy when he allowed Rod and Scunthorpe forward, Lawther, to be both hacked and kicked in a mix up in the Scunthorpe area while Mr Spittle stood and watched. It was not until the ball was cleared that he blew his whistle to allow Rod and the Scunthorpe player to be treated.

The goalmouth scramble resulting in Rod being treated by a trainer, Jimmy Wallbanks

Areff's cartoon report of the match in the Reading Chronicle summarised the game beautifully.

another win... "HANDS DOWN?"

ROY BENTLEY'S CHANGES PAY OFF... AS ROD THORNHILL'S TWO BEAT SCUNTHORPE

IN THE FIRST 15 MINS OF THIS GAME... LITTLE DOUG WEBB INSPIRED MOST ATTACKS AND GOALS SEEMED BOUND TO COME... BUT THE VISITING KEEPER SAVED EVERYTHING PLUS A GREAT SHOT FROM MIKE TRAVERS... BUT HIS SAVE WAS HEADED BACK BY PAT TERRY... FOR ROD THORNHILL TO NOD INTO GOAL!!

READING FELL AWAY AFTER H.T. & IT WAS THE TURN OF THE DEFENCE TO SHINE... THEN A DISPUTED "HANDS" LED TO THE REF CHANGING HIS MIND... & BEFORE WE KNEW WHAT WAS HAPPENING... PAT TERRY WAS RACING DOWN THE LEFT WING ALONE... HE CENTRED PERFECTLY & THERE WAS ROD TO DRIVE IN HIS SECOND GOAL !!!

THIS LED TO AN UGLY INCIDENT IN THE SCUNTHORPE GOAL / IT RESEMBLED A BOXING RING BUT READING HELD ON TO THE LEAD & IN THE END WON "HANDS DOWN"?... JUSTIFYING ROY BENTLEY'S SWEEPING CHANGES... AND JUSTIFYING BETTER SUPPORT THAN 6,726

Four days later, Reading were at home against QPR, this time for an entertaining and eventful Wednesday midweek match.

It all started in the 10th minute, when the QPR goalkeeper, Smith, collided with one of his own players, and after four minutes of treatment, Smith returned to goal with his face heavily plastered.

QPR held out until the 28th minute when Pat Terry rose to head home the first goal. After 35 minutes, Smith collapsed after another goalmouth scramble and had to leave the field for treatment. With an outfield player in goal and down to 10 men, this seemed to urge QPR on, and they equalised after 40 minutes and immediately after scoring, Smith returned in goal.

The second half was even more eventful! Another Pat Terry goal put Reading 2-1 up straight after the break, and then a defensive error saw QPR equalise six minutes later.

It looked like the game was heading for a draw before Reading went up another gear in the closing stages with Terry completing his hat trick after 78 minutes, and then with 5 minutes to go and the fans seemingly celebrating a 3-2 win, Rod made it 4-2 after a pass through the middle from Johnny Petts.

QPR then scored straight from the kick-off to make it 4-2 before Douggie Webb raced through to hit the fifth to seal a 5-3 win.

Roger Ware, the reporter from the Chronicle, had this say about Rod after the game *"I rated Thornhill one of Reading's biggest successes in this memorable affair. He did a tremendous amount of work, covered a tremendous amount of ground, often unnoticed – but caused considerable confusion in Ranger's rear division."*

It may have been that this game took a lot out of the players as 3 days later, they travelled to Walsall, losing 4-1 before hosting QPR again in a midweek League cup fixture.

QPR players and supporters must have been sick of the sight of Reading as Reading cruised to a 4-0 win to take them into the second round.

A few days later, it was back to league duty, and undoubtedly, this game was the highlight of Rod's professional career scoring an incredible 4 goals in the first 29 minutes of the game.

Reading met Watford at Elm Park on 26th September 1964 with Rod still playing in the inside right position, and it took only 11 minutes for Rod to score the first of 4 goals after a Pat Terry shot rebounded off the post for Rod to nod past the helpless Watford keeper.

After 20 minutes, Dennis Allen challenged the Watford keeper who managed to get to the ball first, but he could only play the ball into the path of Rod, who intelligently chipped it over the keeper into the goal from thirty yards out and just seconds later, a Dennis Allen cross was smashed high into the goal by Rod to make it 3-0.

Pat Terry then latched onto a ball in the corner of the Watford area to take it past the keeper and pass to Douggie Webb, who, in turn, passed to Rod for a simple tap in for the fourth goal.

Dick Spiers challenges Ron Saunders of Watford while Rod looks on to the left.

Watford managed to get a goal back just before the first half ended, and then three minutes after the break, they had scored again to make it 4-2. Reading immediately picked up the pace with Dennis Allen scoring the fifth before Mick

Travers rounded off the scoring with the sixth goal in an impressive 6-2 win.

Rod had grabbed the headlines in the Reading Chronicle with "**Hot Shot Rodney Rocks Watford**", and in the Sunday Mirror, Rod was named "**Top shot of the day.**"

The People had a headline of "**Thornhill is Tops-Thanks to Pat Terry**."

It was, in fact, Pat Terry who was named man of the match despite Rod's four goals, for having a hand in 5 of the Reading goals, but it could never take the memory away of scoring 4 goals in one match, in the first 29 minutes of a game.

Rod remembers that his father had decided not to go to this match and was doing some work in his garden at the time Rod was playing. One of Rod's sisters ran out to tell him that Rod had scored 4 goals. His dad didn't believe her and went indoors to put the radio on, but they didn't mention who had scored the goals. When he found out later, he was overjoyed that Rod had scored the 4 goals in one game and was probably cursing the fact that he had missed it!

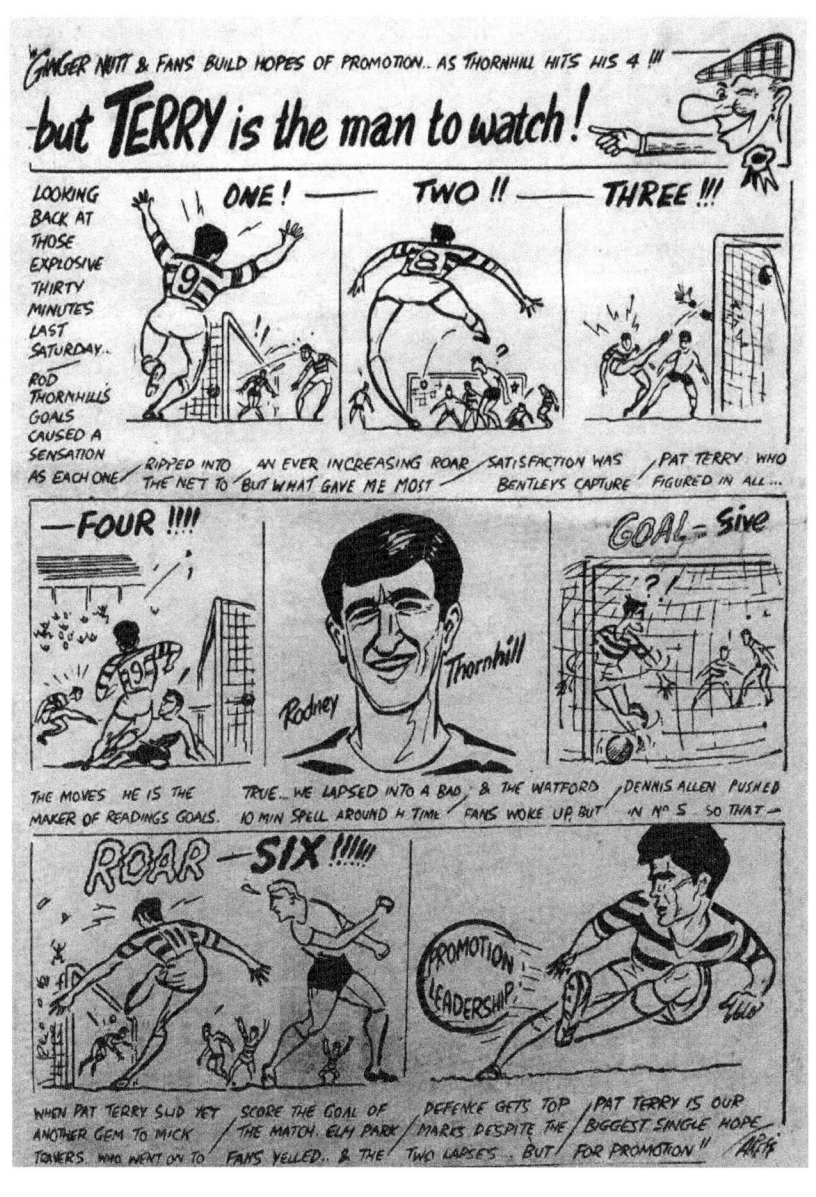

Areff's take on the Watford game from the Reading Chronicle

Rod had now scored seven goals in six games and was now top scorer.

The win against Watford took the team up to fourth place in the table, just one point off the top and looking good for a promotion push this season.

The next game saw Reading visit Bristol City looking to carry on the momentum from the Watford game, and after 30 minutes, Rod had the ball in the back of the city net. Douggie Webb had raced down the right-wing, and his cross looked like it was going in when the City keeper jumped up to keep the ball out, and while he was on the floor, the ball was still in the air. Rod arrived to head the ball home, but the referee disallowed the goal for offside to the disbelief of the players and manager Roy Bentley who commented that *"Doug Webb made sure he played everyone onside by taking the ball almost to the line."*

Bristol City then went 2-0 up before another seemingly good Reading goal was disallowed by the referee for "dangerous kicking" after the City keeper had slipped and dropped the ball into the path of Pat Terry, who put the ball into the net.

A couple more wins and a draw saw Reading sitting in 4th place, one point off the top, before facing first division Fulham in round 3 of the League Cup on 14th October 1964.

With the likes of Bobby Robson, future world cup winner, George Cohen and a young Rodney Marsh playing, with Johnny Haynes ruled out with flu. Reading did well to secure a draw with Rod still playing at inside right. Rod was to miss the replay when Reading would shock Fulham at Craven Cottage with an incredible 3-1 win.

Reading had played Bristol Rovers on the Saturday before the replay with Fulham and had lost 1-0 away. Roy Bentley had considered this game to be a big four-pointer with Rovers on 18 points, the same as Reading, but in third place due to goal difference.

A disappointing 1-0 loss followed with Bentley commenting that *"we had chances after creating openings but failed at the final attempt. Recently this has been our downfall in our away fixtures, and if we are to maintain our league position, these chances must result in goals."*

As a result of the Bristol Rovers game, Rod was dropped for the replay with Fulham and went back to play for the reserves in the Combination League.

Rod in training with Dick Spiers at Prospect Park

Rod did not return to the first team until an FA Cup round 4 replay against first division Burnley on 2nd February 1965, where he came on for the injured Peter Kerr, who had scored the equaliser in a 1-1 draw at Elm Park in the first match.

Reading battled well on a slippery pitch and went close with two chances early on. Reading held out until 5 minutes from time, when the Burnley pressure finally paid off and a goal by Lochhead saw them through to the next round, where they lost 2-1 to Man Utd.

Missing the next match, where Watford gained revenge for the earlier 6-2 defeat by beating Reading 5-1 at Vicarage Road, Rod again returned to first-team action at left half for the home match against Workington Town, which ended in a 1-0 win for Reading.

Before Rod had been dropped, the team were sitting in 4th place. On his recall, though, the team had slipped to 17th place after a poor run of results.

It was Rod's shot that was deflected into the goal by one of the Colchester defenders, which earned them a 1-1 draw on 13th March 1965, although Reading had been on top for most of the game, and this was followed by a 2-1 win over top of the table Carlisle Utd in the next game.

The changes made by Roy Bentley seemed to have steadied the ship, and with 3 wins and 3 draws in the next 6 games, the team rose up the table to 12th place with the chance to move up to 9th place before a visit to the bottom of the table team, Port Vale. On a heavy pitch caused by thawing snow and then rain, Reading struggled to play any constructive football and lost 2-0.

Unfortunate events on 3rd April 1965 saw Reading down to 9 men in the second half against second from bottom Luton Town, after Full Back, Colin Meldrum and Goalkeeper, Arthur Wilkie, had collided in the Reading penalty area. Both had to go off for treatment, with Arthur Wilkie taken to the hospital with a concussion.

Dennis Allen went in goal. Rod remembers that there was no particular plan if the goalkeeper got injured during the game as to who went in goal, only that he did not want to! It was just a matter of who volunteered, and Denis must have volunteered. Rod does remember going in goal once in training for shooting practice but didn't really want to dive around like goalkeepers do. Roy Bentley came up to Rod afterwards and said to him, "Remind me never to put you in goal, Rod!"

Colin Meldrum was patched up and then put in the forward line, where he went onto score 10 minutes before time, but at that time, Reading were already 3-0 down and lost 3-1.

Rod took on a more attacking role, at inside right, in the next game against Exeter City, earning a 2-2 draw, before reverting back to left half in 2-1 win at home to Mansfield.

A Mansfield defender heads the ball away as Rod looks on ready to pounce

Reading finished off the season with a 4-2 win over Peterborough at Elm Park with Rod scoring the fourth goal in the 83rd minute after a Mick Fairchild shot had rebounded off the post into the path of Rod.

Areff's report on the final game of the 1964/65 season

It was a disappointing end to the season for Reading, who had been pushing for a promotion place for the first half of the season but ended up finishing in 13th with the reserves finishing in 15th.

It was a good season for Rod, though. After scoring in the season's final game, he took his goal tally to 8 for the season after making 31 appearances.

1964-65 Division 3 Table

	Team	Pl	W	D	L	F	A	Pts
1	Carlisle Utd (P)	46	25	10	11	76	53	60
2	Bristol City (P)	46	24	11	11	92	55	59
3	Mansfield Town	46	24	11	11	95	61	59
4	Hull City	46	23	12	11	91	57	58
5	Brentford	46	24	9	13	83	55	57
6	Bristol Rovers	46	20	15	11	82	58	55
7	Gillingham	46	23	9	14	70	50	55
8	Peterborough Utd	46	22	7	17	85	74	51
9	Watford	46	17	16	13	71	64	50
10	Grimsby Town	46	16	17	13	68	67	49
11	Bournemouth	46	16	11	17	72	63	47
12	Southend Utd	46	19	8	19	78	71	46
13	**READING**	46	16	14	16	70	70	46
14	QPR	46	17	12	17	72	80	46
15	Workington Town	46	17	12	17	58	69	46
16	Shrewsbury Town	46	15	12	19	76	84	42
17	Exeter City	46	12	17	17	51	52	41
18	Scunthorpe Utd	46	14	12	20	65	72	40
19	Walsall	46	15	7	24	55	80	37
20	Oldham Athletic	46	13	10	23	61	83	36
21	Luton Town (R)	46	11	11	24	51	94	33
22	Port Vale (R)	46	9	14	23	41	76	32
23	Colchester Utd (R)	46	10	10	26	75	50	32
24	Barnsley (R)	46	9	11	28	54	90	29

1964-65 Combination Division 2 Table

	Team	PL	W	D	L	F	A	Pts
1	Southampton Reserves	36	19	11	6	80	58	49
2	Coventry City Reserves	36	20	7	9	96	55	47
3	Swindon Town Reserves	36	21	4	11	84	53	46
4	Oxford Utd Reserves	36	21	4	11	69	51	46
5	Leyton Orient Reserves	36	16	10	10	73	61	42
6	Luton Town Reserves	36	16	10	10	77	68	42
7	Charlton Athletic Reserves	36	15	10	11	71	51	40
8	Birmingham City Reserves	36	15	8	13	76	58	38
9	QPR Reserves	36	14	9	13	54	38	37
10	Brighton Reserves	36	13	10	13	63	59	36
11	Bournemouth Reserves	36	12	12	12	53	51	36
12	Watford Reserves	36	12	10	14	62	67	34
13	Brentford Reserves	36	12	8	16	54	62	32
14	Aldershot Reserves	36	12	8	16	65	74	32
15	**READING RESERVES**	**36**	**10**	**11**	**15**	**64**	**78**	**31**
16	Southend Reserves	36	11	5	20	78	96	27
17	Notts County Reserves	36	7	10	19	53	89	24
18	Bristol Rovers Reserves	36	7	9	20	52	97	23
19	Millwall Reserves	36	6	10	20	37	85	22

SEASON
1964-5

READING

FOOTBALL CLUB
OFFICIAL PROGRAMME 4d

Chapter 6: 1965-66 – Reading Bank on Thornhill

READING: Back Row (from the left), Michael Travers, Rodney Thornhill, Denis Allen, Pat Terry, Michael Dixon, Arthur Wilkie, Maurice Cook, Peter Knight, Dick Spiers. Front Row, Alan Searrott, Gordon Neate, Brian Faulkes, Colin Meldrum, Peter Shreeves, Terry McDonald, Douggie Webb and Maurice Evans.

Reading FC Team Photo – 1965-66

There were some notable changes prior to the 65/66 season commencing for Rod and Reading FC.

Rod and Jan had now been able to purchase a three-bedroomed terraced house in Mortimer for £3,200.

Roy Bentley had decided to ditch the blue and white hoops for a more modern sky-blue kit, although the rising cost of stripes and hoops made in modern, lightweight man-made fibres may have had something to do with the decision as a plain kit compared to a striped/hooped kit could cost as much as £16 more per kit.

A change in the rules meant that each team would be allowed one substitute for injuries only, and Ralph Norton became the first Reading player to come on as a substitute for the injured Peter Shreeves in the first game of the season at home to Watford.

The basic weekly wage Rod was receiving at this time had increased to 14 Pounds, 18 Shillings, and 8 pence which in today's money would be approximately £254. However, with bonuses being paid for winning and getting through cup rounds, Rod received 39 pounds, 9 Shillings, and 8 pence in one particularly good week during this season, the equivalent to approximately £695.

Rod started the first game of the season against Watford in another new position, this time at right half, a position he would hold in the team all season, bar one match against Swindon Town.

It wasn't a good start for the Biscuit Men, losing 2-1, but Rod had obviously impressed someone during the game as Roy Bentley called Rod over in training the following week to say that Watford had made enquiries about signing him. Rod asked Roy what he thought about it, and Roy replied by telling Rod that if he was interested or wanted to talk about it more, they could chat about it. Rod thought for a moment and told Roy that it wouldn't be worth it as he was happy at his home club and wanted to stay. This showed Rod's commitment to the club as there was no talk of how much they were offering or how much more money he could earn. He just simply wanted to continue playing football for Reading. It would not be the last time that Watford would make enquiries over the coming seasons for him, but Rod would never be interested in joining them.

A disappointing start to the season saw Reading with just one win in six games with three draws and two defeats and sitting in 15th place in the league.

In the first round of the Football League Cup, Reading managed a 2-2 draw away to Port Vale. However, Rod had given a penalty away when he brought an opposition player down in the penalty area, which was converted.

Rod made amends in the replay, though, at Elm Park. The Reading Chronicle reporter, Roger Ware, mentioned Rod's performance in his report of the game, *"rarely has Reading's lanky right-half got through so much constructive work and come through so many tackles as he did here."* After the game had gone into extra time, with the score at 0-0, Rod was rewarded with his efforts by scoring from close range in the 100th minute to score the only goal of the game to earn the applause from the Elm Park crowd and secure a second-round tie with Southend Utd.

After a bruising 2-2 with Gillingham in the league, resulting in crowd disturbances, the next game would be against Mansfield at home, and there was a sense of déjà vu for Rod and the rest of the team with the appointment of Rex Spittle as referee. Rod certainly remembered him from the season before against Scunthorpe. He would be again involved in controversy allowing a Mansfield goal to stand after it was clear the Mansfield player had punched the ball into the Reading net. Thankfully, Reading were already two up at this stage, but it did not prevent crowd disturbances for the second match in a row, with Mr. Spittle escorted off the pitch by the police at the end of the game.

The second round of the League Cup saw Reading at home to Southend Utd, and the team provided a feast for the fans, winning 5-1 with the fans spilling onto the pitch after the game to mob their Reading heroes!

An impressive 3-3 with Hull City followed with the Evening post commenting that Rod was in terrific form, but it was again tinged with controversy after a Hull player raced through with the score at 3-2 to score an equaliser, but the Linesman had already been holding up his flag for offside as he raced through. The referee consulted the lineman but allowed the goal to stand. As a result of the 3-3 draw, the team moved up to 12th position at the end of September, only 4 points of the top and looking to challenge for a promotion place.

The optimism was short-lived with a poor run of form in the league in October resulting in defeats against local rivals, Oxford 0-1, Walsall 0-3, Bournemouth 2-3, and a 1-1 draw with Workington after which Roy Bentley commented that *"it was most disappointing for everyone for points are badly needed just now, and I am at a loss to understand this complete contrast of form in a matter of three days."*

The three days he was referring to was the third-round League cup tie away to second division Derby County, where they had put in a tremendous performance to earn a well-deserved 1-1 draw with the Evening Post commenting, *"Thornhill turning on another of those outstanding displays he seems to keep for away matches in top form"* and *"Meldrum, Thornhill and McDonald were the stars."*

The replay at Elm Park was even better for Reading thanks to their *"skill and superiority"* with an impressive 2-0 win to take them into round four.

Reading ended October with a 1-0 win over Southend and a booking for Rod. Reading were now sitting in 17th place and needed a good run of form in November to push them back up the table.

A 5-1 defeat in the League cup against Cardiff City on t3rd November 1965 was followed by a 5-0 defeat away to Swindon on 6th November, and with Dick Spiers dropped, Rod was moved back to play at centre half for this game.

81

After the game, Assistant Manager Jimmy Wheeler reported, "I thought Rod had a shaky start, but then did well to keep the Swindon centre forward out of the game." However, it was not the best start to November, and things had to change.

Roy Bentley decided to organise a trial match before the first round FA Cup match with Rod and Dick Spiers both playing at centre half and Roy Bentley, playing for the opposition to get a close-up look at them both in action!

Dick Spiers was recalled to centre back, and Rod reverted back to right wing half for the FA Cup match with Bristol Rovers, which resulted in a much needed 3-2 win after a Denis Allen goal two minutes from time and with Spider working his magic, he was described by the Chronicle as *"virtually blotting out the menace of Rover's top scorer, Bobby Jones."*

A 3-3 draw against Grimsby and a 2-0 home win against Brentford saw the team picking up some form at the end of November despite still being in 17th place in the league.

Despite the improvement in form in November, December started with a report that Reading were willing to buy and sell, with Roy Bentley given £10,000 to purchase new players. This didn't faze the players, though, who carried on their good form at the end of November by thrashing Brentford 5-0 at home in the FA Cup second round to set up a tantalising third-round tie against First Division Sheffield Wednesday.

Reading carried on the good form with a 3-0 home win against York City with Rod and other Wing Half, Maurice Evans, repeatedly going up with the forwards to help pierce a stubborn York defence.

York in red, clear off the line as Rod, left of picture, looks eagerly on towards the left of picture

The last of game 1965 saw Reading at home to Peterborough Utd on 27th December and Rod in his usual position of the right half.

On a slippery, frost-covered pitch, the match was scrappy, with Peterborough mastering the conditions in the first half and twice hitting the post. Reading came out the better team in the second half but went a goal behind. It was only a short-lived lead as Reading equalised shortly afterwards through Dennis Allen.

With only four minutes of the game, the ball was flicked on by Dougie Webb, and *"Rodney Spider Thornhill stretched his 6ft frame to head the winner."*

The Evening Post led with the headline *"THORNHILL TO THE RESCUE WITH LATE WINNER"* and reported, *"If the wing-half had been able to select the day and the minute of his first goal of the season, he could not have picked a more opportune moment.*

Rod, far left, scores the second goal against Peterborough Utd after a flick on by Douggie Webb from a corner.

Rod finished off 1965 with his first goal in the league, appearing in all league and cup matches so far in the season and the birth of a baby daughter, Jane, born on 14th December.

In what would be an exciting year for English football, 1966 also started well for Rod with a 3-0 home win over Walsall on 3rd January 1966 and Rod drawing high praise from the Evening Post reporter: *'Rod Thornhill was outstanding, and I think it is about time he was given credit for what he is – one of the most awkward defenders to fool."*

Reading had now won their last seven home games in a row and had not lost over the previous seven games.

They extended their unbeaten a week later with a 3-3 draw away to Shrewsbury. However, it was a match, they should have won, having taken the lead three times in the match, but it was still good form going into the big FA Cup round 3 matches against Sheffield Wednesday on 22nd January 1966.

However, there were considerable doubts about whether the cup match would go ahead with a big freeze hitting the country at the start of the week.

Roy Bentley discusses the pitch conditions with a local referee whilst the first team continue to train on the Elm Park pitch.

Fortunately, after hours of digging, raking and rolling by the ground staff, the match referee declared the pitch was fit to play.

In a pulsating match, Reading battled well against their First Division opponents in front of a crowd of 22,500 but went in at halftime 1-0 down. With Roy Bentley's half time talk still ringing in their ears, the team mounted a stream of attacks, and it resulted in an equaliser as described by the Reading Evening Post reporter:

"The first came from Rod Thornhill, a player I have criticised a lot in the past, but who has proved in the last couple of months that he is now both a first-class man when it comes to linking with an attack. And he'll never score a finer goal than on Saturday. Slicing through a for once hesitant Wednesday defence, Thornhill angled the ball across to Douggie Webb, and 22,000 Reading fans held their breath as the accurate return pass suddenly left Rod face to face with England goalkeeper Ron Springett. There was no one else to beat, and Springett groped in vain as the Reading wing-half coolly steered the ball into the net. It was a brilliant goal, and whatever happened afterwards, Reading knew they were not disgraced."

Rod scores the equaliser against Sheffield Wednesday

Sheffield Wednesday were to go 2-1 up, but Reading were still fighting to stay in the game and grabbed an equaliser through Maurice Evans with only six minutes to go, and it seemed a trip to Hillsborough would be Reading's reward. But with only two minutes left, Wednesday would score a fluke goal to break Reading hearts when a cross bounced off a Sheffield Wednesday player's head high into the air, and it looked to be going over the bar, but with goalkeeper Mike Dixon, stranded off his line, the ball somehow nestled in the corner of the Reading net with the Reading defenders standing in despair wondering just how it had gone in.

Areff's report on the Sheffield Wednesday game

Despite the loss in the cup, Reading finished off January with a 2-1 win away to Watford in a match where, apart from the opening 10-minute spell of the game, Reading were always in control.

Reading were still only sitting in 16th place, but with 4 games in hand over some of the other sides above them, if they were able to win all the games in hand, it would take them within 3 points of third place.

February started with a home match against Scunthorpe on 5th February 1965 with a headline in the Evening Post of *READING BANK ON THORNHILL*, and the report went onto state; *"Rod 'Spider' Thornhill takes the field today as Readings, key man. Rod, one of the star performers in the Reading defence in recent weeks, lines up against former Elm Park man Brian Bedford and on the outcome of the battle between these two can rest the result of the whole match."*

On a rainy and windy day, it was Rod who would get the better of the Scunthorpe player with Bedford, *"never escaping the clutches of Rod throughout the game even denying them a shock lead by clearing off the line in the first 10 minutes."* Two Reading goals in the second half gave them a 2-0 win.

Two 1-1 draws against Brighton and high flying Millwall, thanks to some goalkeeping heroics from young Millwall keeper Alex Stepney, meant that at the end of February, Reading had not been beaten in the league for 10 games in a run that stretched back to their last defeat on 6th November 1965. It had moved the team up to 12th place in the league with games in hand which, if they could win, would take them within a point of third place.

March was a busy month for the Biscuit Men with 8 matches scheduled, and it started with a difficult trip to leaders Millwall on 5th March 1965, who would bring Reading's unbeaten run to an abrupt end with a 3-0 win.

Reading were back on track briefly with a 1-0 home win over Bournemouth and then a 2-0 away win at Mansfield before a disappointing 1-0 home defeat by Hull, who were busy exchanging places with Millwall at the top of the table.

There followed a crazy period of 5 games in just 10 days for Reading, starting on 23rd March away to Gillingham. It didn't start well with Reading going into the break 2-0 down, but whatever Roy Bentley said at halftime must have worked as Reading came out for the second half and hit four goals in 19 minutes to win the game 4-2.

A disappointing 2-0 away defeat to local rivals Oxford Utd followed 3 days later on 26th March with Roy Bentley calling the performance *"diabolical"* but with only a two-day rest, Reading faced Peterborough on 28th March and this time, after a 0-0 draw, Bentley was full of praise calling it a *"tremendous performance."*

The players were digging deep now, and although '*not a great game to watch*", according to Bentley, they were still able to record a 3-2 home win over lowly Oldham and lift the team to 10th in the table.

But the strain of so many matches in a short period of time was starting to show, and 2 days later, on 1st April 1965, they suffered a 2-0 home defeat to Swindon Town. Reading had now lost all their matches against local rivals Swindon and Oxford.

A 0-0 draw against Bristol Rovers was followed by an extraordinary 5-4 defeat away to Swansea when Reading had been 3-0 up after 25 minutes. They conceded two just before the break before Reading had scored again just after halftime to make it 4-2 and seemingly had done enough to win the game, but with a lack of concentration and defensive errors creeping in, Swansea scored three times in the last half-hour with talisman Welsh international, Ivor Allchurch, scoring two to secure an unlikely 5-4 win.

By a twist of fate, the teams met just two days later, with Reading gaining revenge with a 2-1 win. This time, Ivor Allchurch, was to have less influence on the game, with Rod blotting out the famed international.

A 1-1 away draw with Brentford was followed by a 2-1 away against an Exeter City side, fighting to stay up. A disappointing 1-0 home defeat to Bristol Rovers on the 29/4/66 saw the team sitting in 12th place.

May started with a break to league action and a testimonial match for Maurice Evans against the 'International Club' made up of ex pros, with Maurice Edelstone, Bobby Campbell and Sammy Chung returning as ex-players and Roy Bentley playing on the left wing. The International team came out on top in an entertaining 4-3 win.

10 BAYLIS SUPERMARKETS

offer YOU quality, value & the best choice in town

we give fabulous GREEN SHIELD STAMPS DOUBLE stamps every Tuesday

READING: BROAD STREET, Erleigh Road and 250 Shinfield Road
CAVERSHAM: 2 Church Street
TILEHURST: School Road

High Street CROWTHORNE
Grove Street WANTAGE
Northbrook Street NEWBURY
Ock Street ABINGDON
High Street WALLINGFORD

Reading

Shirts: Sky Blue
Knickers: Sky Blue

RIGHT   LEFT

Michael Dixon
1

2   Brian Faulkes   3   Colin Meldrum

4   Rodney Thornhill   5   Dick Spiers   6   Maurice Evans

7 Alan Scarrott   Denis Allen 8   9 Peter Silvester   Douggie Webb 10   11 Ian Maidment

REFEREE:
Mr. A. G. Hitchman
(Berks & Bucks F.A.)

Today's Match Ball kindly donated by THE WEST READING LAUNDRY LIMITED

HIGGS — WINES SPIRITS BEERS — DELIVERED TO YOUR HOME — TEL READING 53681

LINESMEN:
RED FLAG—
Mr. M. H. D. Baker
(Berks & Bucks F.A.)
YELLOW FLAG—
Mr. S. Tinsley
(Berks & Bucks F.A.)

Roy Bentley 11   10 Sammy Chung   John Charles 9   8 Maurice Edelston   Bobby Campbell 7

Jimmy Scoular 6   Neil Franklin 5   Bill McGarry 4

Pat Sayward 3   1   Bob Stokoe 2

Dave Underwood

LEFT
Shirts: White
Knickers: White

RIGHT

International Club

kick off with **Huntley & Palmers** Cornish Wafers – at any time!
(always top of the table)

The programme for Reading v International Club

It was back to league action next, with the team travelling up north to play York City on 6th May and Workington Town on 9th May.

© *Mirrorpix/Reach Licensing - Rod, centre right, laughing on the coach outside Elm Park for the northern away trip.*

A good 2-1 win at York was followed by a disappointing 1-0 defeat at Workington with the Evening Post reporting that '*The only Reading players to emerge from the game with much credit were strong men in defence, Dick Spiers and Rod Thornhill."*

The defeat meant they were now 7 points behind third-placed QPR, which would be Reading's next opponents. A well-earned 2-1 victory saw Reading do the double over their higher placed opponents.

Two 4-1 home victories against Exeter City and Shrewsbury Town, with the team playing some attractive football in both games, saw the team rocket up the league to 8th place, just one point behind QPR. Sadly, promotion was not a possibility as Hull and Millwall had already built up a 12-point gap to secure promotion, but Reading still had a chance to finish a very commendable third.

The last home game of the season was against Grimsby Town on 23rd May 1966, and despite pounding the Grimsby Town goal for 90 minutes, the match finished 0-0, so all that was left was an away match at Southend Utd with a chance to finish 4th in the table.

After going a goal down, Rod unleashed a fierce shot that Dennis Allen deflected in to go in at halftime 1-1. Southend scored another in the second half, and despite hitting the bar, Reading could not muster anything in reply. The match did mark an achievement for Rod, though, as he appeared in his 46th consecutive appearance, the only ever-present player this season with the Reading Evening Post commenting that *"Thornhill has been a model of consistency and has probably been Reading's reliable, if not spectacular, performer.'*

At least there was the 1966 World Cup to look forward to!

Rod was an ever-present for the 1965-66 season, playing in all 46 league and cup games. He had also scored 1 goal in the league and 2 in the cup.

The team finally finished in 8th place, with the reserves winning the combination league, although Rod was not to play any reserve games this season.

1965-66 Division 3 Table

	Team	Pl	W	D	L	F	A	Pts
1	Hull City (P)	46	31	7	8	109	62	69
2	Millwall (P)	46	27	11	8	76	43	65
3	QPR	46	24	9	13	95	65	59
4	Scunthorpe Utd	46	21	11	14	80	67	53
5	Workington Town	46	19	14	13	67	57	52
6	Gillingham	46	22	8	16	62	54	52
7	Swindon Town	46	19	13	14	74	48	51
8	**READING**	**46**	**19**	**13**	**14**	**70**	**63**	**51**
9	Walsall	46	20	10	16	77	64	50
10	Shrewsbury Town	46	19	11	16	73	64	49
11	Grimsby Town	46	17	13	16	68	62	47
12	Watford	46	17	13	16	55	51	47
13	Peterborough Utd	46	17	12	17	80	66	46
14	Oxford Utd	46	19	8	19	70	74	46
15	Brighton	46	16	11	19	67	65	43
16	Bristol Rovers	46	14	14	18	64	64	42
17	Swansea Town	46	15	11	20	81	96	41
18	Bournemouth	46	13	12	21	38	56	38
19	Mansfield Town	46	15	8	23	59	89	38
20	Oldham Athletic	46	12	13	21	55	81	37
21	Southend Utd (R)	46	16	4	26	54	83	36
22	Exeter City (R)	46	12	11	23	53	79	35
23	Brentford (R)	46	10	12	24	48	69	32
24	York City (R)	46	9	9	28	53	106	27

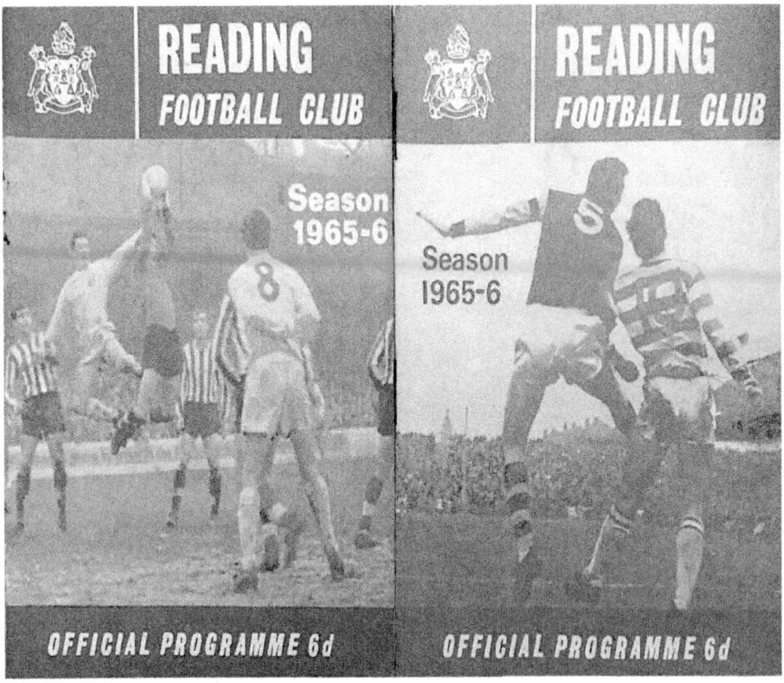
READING
FOOTBALL CLUB
Season
1965-6
OFFICIAL PROGRAMME 6d
READING
FOOTBALL CLUB
Season
1965-6
OFFICIAL PROGRAMME 6d

Chapter 7: 1966-67 - Mr. Versatility

Reading FC Team Photo - 1966-67 – Rod on back row, far left.

While the euphoria of England winning the World Cup was still settling, matters were once again turning to the new season with Roy Bentley aiming to play a 4-3-3 formation, the same formation that England had played in the World Cup.

He had a warning for Rod and the rest of the squad though ahead of the new season *"First team men of last season do not necessarily step straight back in this time, and I shall want to see how everyone shapes up in the coming weeks of training before deciding about the senior side."*

With the signing of 3 new players, Ron Foster, John Chapman and George Harris, hopes were high after a 3-1 victory over second division Cardiff City at Elm Park in a pre-season friendly.

Pre-season training at Elm Park – Rod in dark top nearest the camera

The first game of the league season saw Reading away to newly-promoted Torquay Utd, with Rod surviving the Bentley pre-season warning and taking up his wing-half position in the number 6 jersey.

On a hot and sunny August afternoon, Torquay acclimatised better to the conditions and took the two points with a resounding 3-0 victory.

After drawing 1-1 with Watford in the League Cup, Reading drew 1-1 again, this time against Brighton in a league fixture. Reading had gone 1-0 up in the game after Rod had shot through a crowd of defenders, and a new signing, Ron Foster, had hooked the ball into the Brighton goal. Reading were then caught with too many players upfront and were caught on the break for Brighton to equalise.

Reading's next game in the league was against Darlington, and Roy Bentley explained in the Reading Evening Post how his players would be getting to the Darlington ground, which I doubt we would see these days! *"It's always difficult knowing what to do for the best in the case of a long journey like this one, but the train service is so good that we can even be back in Reading before midnight. We'll arrive in Darlington at 1:40, and I'll make the players walk the two miles over to the ground to get some exercise."*

The two-mile walk to the ground obviously didn't affect the players too much, though, as Reading secured a 1-0 away win despite pressure from Darlington in the second half.

After a 2-1 defeat at Bristol Rovers, Reading were up against one of the pre-season favourites to go up, QPR, and it was looking like things were finally beginning to click with Reading going into halftime at 2-0.

It was going well for Reading until Rod tripped Rodney Marsh in what looked like to be outside the area, but the referee gave a penalty instead, which was converted by QPR. With 11 minutes to go, QPR got their equaliser, and the match ended 2-2.

Rod always enjoyed the banter he had with Rodney Marsh when they played against each other. Whenever he saw he was up against Rod, Marsh would come over and ask Rod, "Are you going to let me score today, Rod?" and Rod would always reply, "Not today, Marshy!"

Rod rates Rodney Marsh as one of the best players he played against in his career, along with Jimmy Greaves, who Rod had to mark in a reserve game when he was playing for Tottenham Hotspur. Greaves was returning from injury, and Rod remembers that he was so quick and tricky that it was difficult to keep up with him due to his movement, but he felt he did a good job!

Rod was also fortunate to mark one of his childhood heroes, Stanley Matthews, in an exhibition game. Matthews was coming towards the end of his career, but he was still tricky with the ball. Rod did try talking to him during the game, but he wasn't interested in chatting at the time!

After the QPR game, although it was a much better performance, the team had only secured 4 points and sat in 18th place. Roy Bentley looked set to abandon the 4-3-3 for a more orthodox formation they had been used to as he felt the players were either unable or unwilling to apply themselves to the new formation. Rod remembers Roy changing the formation a few times, but he was always willing to play anyway; Bentley wanted him to play, but he does remember a few players struggled in a new formation.

After defeating Watford 1-0 in the League Cup replay, they were drawn against first division Leicester City with England World Cup hero Gordon Banks in goal, and he was in fine form again with some world-class saves to keep a clean sheet in a 5-0 drubbing of Reading.

Rod was called upon to play centre half for the home match against Darlington on 21st September 1966, after the centre half, Dick Spiers was injured, and then a replacement, Ray Dean, was ruled out with an injury on the afternoon of the game. The versatile Rod was called upon and did well to hold off the Darlington forward line, with Reading keeping a clean sheet in a 1-0 win. Roy Bentley was pleased with Rod's performance and commented *"Thornhill did an excellent job as stand-in centre half."*

Rod had no problem with fitting in at the centre half and just enjoyed playing in any position.

It was back to a more usual role for Rod in the next game as he resumed his position at wing-half for a 2-1 home win over Swindon before a 2-1 defeat against Bristol Rovers.

The inconsistent form continued into October with a moral boosting 3-1 away win against local rivals Oxford Utd, before the predictable 3-2 defeat at home to Colchester, described by Bentley as a *'shambles'* and resulted in 4 changes for the next game against Shrewsbury Town on 15th October 1966 with Rod one of the players that was dropped although Bentley commented that Rod had been rested more than dropped for the game *"He'd played a lot of games in succession and had lost a bit of bite from his play. I think he was glad of a day off, and I hope he'll come back all the better for it."*

Missing the Shrewsbury Town match brought an end to an 82 successive appearance run for Rod, stretching from 13/2/64 to 15/10/66. Rod would only be out for one game following the 1-0 defeat to Shrewsbury as he was recalled for the next game, a 2-0 defeat to Grimsby despite an injury scare prior to the game. The injury would come back to haunt

Rod in a 0-0 draw with Middlesbrough, limping off after 60 minutes of the game.

It would be a disappointing end to October, with a 5-2 away defeat by bottom club Swansea Town, which saw Reading fourth from bottom with 11 points.

The start of November saw a 0-0 draw with Bournemouth, and Reading had now scored just twice in 5 games.

Reading doubled that tally in the next game against Leyton Orient with Rod scoring from a flashing header and also marking danger man Cliff Holton out of the game. But despite Reading scoring two and Rod having a shot cleared off the line, it wasn't enough to win the game, losing 3-2, but there were glimpses of improvement.

In an attempt to change things around and to give new signing Ernie Yard a chance to settle in with his new teammates, Roy Bentley arranged a trial match before the next home game to Grimsby Town and used this as an opportunity to try Rod in attack, commenting *"Rod did very well indeed in that position and has certainly earned a chance there tomorrow."*

The move to the inside right worked well for Rod and Reading as they cruised to an ill-tempered 6-0 home win over Grimsby, with Rod scoring 2 cracking goals in the 20th and 28th minute.

© Mirrorpix/Reach Licensing - Rod fires in Reading's third against Grimsby.

After a 2-1 home win over Gillingham 3 days later, it was the turn of the first round of the FA Cup with a tricky away tie to non-league Hendon, who were built up as possible giant killers.

Reading put paid to their giant killer plans with 2 goals in the first 16 minutes of the game. It took Reading only two minutes to score through George Harris before a Pat Terry shot rebounded off the crossbar into the path of Rod, who coolly finished for Reading's second. George Harris then supplied a low cross for Rod to hammer in on the run to go into halftime at 3-0 up.

Hendon scored a consolation goal in the second half from a goalmouth scramble, and Rod nearly completed his hat trick just before the end of the game but for a full length save from the Hendon keeper.

Reading were comfortably through to the second round.

Areff's report of the Hendon match

At the end of November, the team had moved up to 16th in the league, and Rod had scored 5 in the month after moving to the inside left and had Roy Bentley singing his

109

praises, *"Rod's form had had as much to do with our recent success as anybody. He has got through a lot of work, both positioning himself in attack and running back in defence. This is what opponents don't expect, players to come back as hard as Rod does."*

With Roy Bentley's words of praise still ringing in Rod's ears, it was only a minute into the game when Rod scored the first goal against Scunthorpe at home on 3rd December 1966 after a mix up between Scunthorpe keeper, Ray Clemence and a defender, gave Rod an open goal. Three more goals gave Reading a convincing 4-0 win.

Scunthorpe keeper, Ray Clemence, saves from the waiting Rod.

Reading travelled to Oldham for the next game and inflicted their first home defeat of the season with a 3-1 win at Boundary Park, which Roy Bentley described as *"one of our best games this season and well-deserved victory in which each and every one gave their best."*

A fifth successive win, with a 2-1 win over Torquay, even gave the manager some optimism to mention promotion, with Bentley saying that the *"odds against must be enormous, it is certainly not too late.*

A break from the league and cup saw Reading entertaining a showbiz eleven for charity on 14/12/1966, which resulted in a 10-10 draw with Rod scoring three of the goals!!

10 BAYLIS
SUPERMARKETS THROUGHOUT BERKSHIRE

OFFER YOU... & Green Shield Stamps
1 STOP SHOPPING (DOUBLE ON TUESDAYS)

Reading

Shirts: Sky Blue
Knickers: Sky Blue

RIGHT

Arthur Wilkie
1

LEFT

Dave Bacuzzi
2

Colin Meldrum
3

Ernie Yard
4

Ray Dean
5

John Chapman
6

Alan Scarrott
7

Denis Allen
8

Pat Terry
9

Rod Thornhill
10

George Harris
11

REFEREE:
Mr. N. A. S. Matthews
(Oxon F.A.)

Today's Match Ball
kindly donated by
Messrs. H. F. WARNER
LIMITED
Knowl Hill, Reading

WINES SPIRITS BEERS
HIGGS
DELIVERED TO YOUR HOME
TEL READING 53681

LINESMEN:
RED FLAG
Mr. A. G. Hitchman
(Berks and Bucks F.A.)

YELLOW FLAG
Mr. P. G. Farrow
(Berks and Bucks F.A.)

Brian Close
11

Len Ducquemin
10

Tommy Steele
7

Danny Blanchflower
9

Jimmy Tarbuck
8

Ken Jones
6

Billy Wright
5

Peter Thompson
4

Ziggy Jackson
3

Jimmy Henney
2

LEFT

Jess Conrad
1

RIGHT

Show Biz XI

CUP WINNERS!

Huntley & Palmers
butter osborne

Showbiz 11 program

© Mirrorpix/Reach Licensing - Rod marks star of stage, Tommy Steele

Reading's run was finally over on Boxing Day with a 3-1 defeat away to Walsall in a stormy encounter, but they were to gain revenge the following day, reversing the scoreline at Elm Park, and it was Rod opening the scoring from close range after just two minutes after a cross by Pat Terry. Walsall grabbed an equaliser after 14 minutes before Pat Terry scored in the 33rd and 70th minute to win the game for Reading.

1966 ended with a 1-0 away win to Brighton and 7 league wins in 8 games, which took the team up to 11th place in the league, looking good to push on in the New Year.

The average attendance at Elm Park for this season stood at 6,518, which saw them 15th out of 24 teams.

An enforced break due to freezing weather didn't see Reading return to action until 14th January 1967 with a difficult trip to leaders QPR and chief goal scorer Pat Terry suspended for this match.

Roy Bentley was looking for someone to replace him in the centre forward role, and after Bentley had seen Rod "*play very well*" in a practice match, scoring two goals, he felt that Rod "*was the man for the job*". He must have also been swayed by the fact that since Rod had moved to Inside Left, Reading had only lost once in nine league and cup games.

It was always going to be a difficult game against the eventual champions of the league, and although Rod had won a penalty, the penalty was missed by George Harris, and Reading went down 2-1.

Rod was playing centre forward for the next game against lower league opposition Aldershot in the 2nd round of the FA Cup, but he was unable to repeat his two-goal performance in the first round at Hendon, and despite Rod hitting the post, it was a 1-0 win for Aldershot to take them through to the next round.

Watford were the next visitors to Elm Park, with Rod switching back to Inside Left and after half an hour of the game, Rod had risen to head Reading into a 1-0 lead from a corner before Watford equalised on the stroke of halftime.

Rod, centre, puts Reading 1-0 up against Watford with a header.

Reading thought they had the winner in the 70th minute when Rod's pass had found Ron Foster, who thought he had scored, but the referee ruled it out for an earlier infringement even though it looked as though he had allowed play to continue.

The match finished 1-1, but not without a scare as Colin Meldrum looked as though he had handled the ball in the Reading area, but luckily, the referee did not see it.

Areff's cartoon report of the 1-1 draw with Watford in the Reading Chronicle

Reading then visited Swindon Town, who had just beaten first division, West Ham, in the FA Cup and with the Reading Evening Post commenting that *"Reading's forward line was at times playing first-class football"* Reading came away with a well-deserved 1-0 win. The performance won the UWIN team of the week award, where the prize was for the local youth team to be presented with a brand-new kit. The team chosen by Reading FC captain, Colin Meldrum, was a youth team based in Shinfield, who had not won a game all season.

Confidence was high after a win over their local rivals, and it was another local rival in the form of Oxford Utd, who they would play next at home.

Reading started off well when Rod's cross was nearly turned into the Oxford net by one of their own defenders. A few minutes later, Reading were one up going into halftime.

Reading came out quickly for the second half, and straight away, Rod was denied a goalscoring chance by a good tackle from an Oxford defender. Oxford then equalised and piled on the pressure. Rod was again involved, saving a certain goal, after the Reading keeper, Wilkie, had lost the ball in a goalmouth scramble, and Rod had cleared for a corner.

Reading, though, couldn't hold out and a goal in the 79th minute won the game for Oxford.

Rod gets up to head against Oxford Utd with Ron Atkinson (no 4) looking on

With Roy Bentley describing the performance as "*absolutely terrible*", it was inevitable that Bentley would make changes for the next game at Mansfield, and despite travelling up with the team for a 4-2 defeat, Rod was left out of the side and would not regain a place in the side for the rest of the season.

For the rest of the season, Rod would be named as an occasional unused substitute for the first team while playing regularly for the reserves, who were bottom of the Combination League.

With the reserves looking to add a much-needed punch to the attack, it was Rod they turned to lead the line of attack against Notts Forest Reserves, and it was Rod's goal against them in a 2-1 win which gave them their first win in a month on 3rd April 1967.

However, it was not enough to stop the reserves from finishing bottom of the Combination league. The first team were to finish an agonizing 4th place at the end of the season, just two points off a promotion place.

Although Rod had not played for the first team since 11th February 1967, he still finished 6th in the most appearances of the season in League and Cup with 33 appearances, and he finished the 5th top scorer with 8 goals.

1966-67 Division 3 Table

	Team	Pl	W	D	L	F	A	Pts
1	QPR (P)	46	26	15	5	103	38	67
2	Middlesbrough (P)	46	23	9	14	87	64	55
3	Watford	46	20	14	12	61	46	54
4	**READING**	**46**	**22**	**9**	**15**	**76**	**57**	**53**
5	Bristol Rovers	46	20	13	13	76	67	53
6	Shrewsbury Town	46	20	12	14	77	62	52
7	Torquay Utd	46	19	13	14	74	48	51
8	Swindon Town	46	20	10	16	81	59	50
9	Mansfield Town	46	20	9	17	84	79	49
10	Oldham Athletic	46	19	10	17	80	63	48
11	Gillingham	46	15	16	15	58	62	46
12	Walsall	46	18	10	18	65	72	46
13	Colchester Utd	46	17	10	19	76	73	44
14	Orient	46	13	18	15	58	68	44
15	Peterborough Utd	46	14	15	17	66	71	43
16	Oxford Utd	46	15	13	18	61	66	43
17	Grimsby Town	46	17	9	20	61	68	43
18	Scunthorpe Utd	46	17	8	21	58	73	42
19	Brighton	46	13	15	18	61	71	41
20	Bournemouth	46	12	17	17	39	57	41
21	Swansea Town (R)	46	12	15	19	85	89	39
22	Darlington (R)	46	13	11	22	47	81	37
23	Doncaster Rovers (R)	46	12	8	26	58	117	32
24	Workington Town (R)	46	12	7	27	55	89	31

1966-67 Combination Division 1 Table

	Team	PL	W	D	L	F	A	Pts
1	Tottenham Reserves	34	23	3	6	83	31	49
2	Arsenal Reserves	34	18	4	10	60	41	40
3	Swindon Town Reserves	34	16	6	10	48	45	38
4	Peterborough Utd Res	34	15	7	10	66	61	37
5	Southampton Reserves	34	15	6	11	66	45	36
6	West Ham Reserves	34	15	6	11	63	46	36
7	Leicester City Reserves	34	13	8	11	61	545	34
8	Notts Forest Reserves	34	14	5	13	52	55	33
9	Coventry City Reserves	34	13	6	13	56	64	32
10	Northampton Town Res	34	14	3	15	56	60	31
11	Chelsea Reserves	34	11	6	15	58	77	28
12	Plymouth Argyle Reserves	34	11	5	16	60	58	27
13	Gillingham Reserves	34	11	5	16	49	71	27
14	Ipswich Town Reserves	34	10	6	16	43	53	26
15	Crystal Palace Reserves	34	11	4	17	51	71	26
16	Fulham Reserves	34	9	6	17	48	60	24
17	**READING RESERVES**	34	8	4	20	41	78	20

READING
FOOTBALL CLUB

Season 1966-7

FOOTBALL LEAGUE—DIV. III
SATURDAY, 5th NOVEMBER
BOURNEMOUTH

OFFICIAL PROGRAMME 6d

Chapter 8: 1967-68 - Ace in the Pack

READING: Back row—Scarrott, Allen, Harris, Silvester, Dean, Thornhill. Centre-row—Lamble, Hitchcock, Bishton, Bayliss, Wilkie, Smee, Drumm, Spiers. Front-row—Johnson, Foster, Mullen, Meldrum, Wheeler, Chapman, Bacuzzi.

Reading FC Team Photo - 1967-68

In the summer during pre-season, Rod remembers that the club directors would sometimes ask some of the players if they wanted to earn extra cash by doing a few odd jobs, and he remembers one summer being asked to paint a row of houses on St Barnabus Road in Shinfield with 5 or 6 of the other players. Like Rod, some of the other players would have second jobs with one or two painter decorators in the side, and goalkeeper, Mike Dixon, would be busy running his own newsagent when not training or playing.

Apart from this, according to Rod, the players didn't have much to do with the directors. He did though, strike up a friendship with Duncan Vincent, who owned an auctioneering house and an estate agency. As he knew Rod was working as a French polisher in the afternoons, he would always get Rod to do some French polishing or furniture repairs. Duncan would also come in the dressing room before and after the game, but the other directors wouldn't have much to do with the players and would generally keep away from them.

The relationship carried on when Rod returned to the area in 1980, and Duncan would always be coming around with odd jobs to do. You always knew when Duncan Vincent was on the way as you could hear his big booming voice before you saw him!

Rod remembers Fred May was the secretary at the time and was the one who called the YMCA to tell Rod to get to the ground to sign as an amateur. The other directors Rod remembers are Alfie Smith, who owned Smith Coaches. They would sometimes use his coaches on away matches, and Mr Baylis, who owned a grocery shop with a few branches in Reading, but there didn't seem to be many people on the board compared to other clubs.

All the current squad of players had been re-signed by the beginning of July 1967 and the squad set about the most challenging schedule of pre-season ever imposed on the club, including two full weeks of full-day training at

Easthampstead Sports Centre, which included cross country and track running, weight training and ball practice.

Reading FC were also looking for new places to train and had struck up a deal with the Reading Stadium greyhound owners, situated off the Oxford Road in Tilehurst, to train on the centre green on the basis that the club would maintain the grass.

On the pitch, Roy Bentley was looking at the best formation to use for the coming season and was changing between 4-2-4 to 4-3-3 for a series of pre-season friendlies.

As far as Rod was concerned, he did not play in any of the pre-season games and started the season as an unused substitute for the first couple of games.

Rod was again named as a substitute for the first round of the League Cup at home to Bristol Rovers, and within a few minutes of coming on, he had won a penalty after being pushed in the area. The penalty was converted to complete a 3-0 win. The win secured Reading a second-round tie with West Brom.

An injury at the start of September delayed any chance of getting back into the team for Rod. In a report from the Reading Evening Post, it appeared that Rod was on his way back to solve an injury crisis ahead of the upcoming game against Northampton with a headline of "Versatile Thornhill is the man to solve Reading's problem." It wasn't to be as Rod himself failed a late fitness test before the game.

A few days later, it was again reported that Rod was in the frame for a recall to the side for the next round of the League Cup against first division West Brom.

Spider – Back in contention for the West Brom match?

It wasn't to be as injury again prevented Rod from playing in the West Brom game when Reading surprised their Division 1 opponents by winning 3-1.

Rod was fit enough to play for the reserves on 20th September 1967 against Cardiff Reserves. Then a substitute appearance followed a week later for the first team in a 0-0 draw with Shrewsbury Town despite being sent home ill a few days earlier.

After another brief appearance as a sub in a 2-1 defeat away to Oxford and with the team lying in 3rd place in the league, it was the turn of Arsenal in the 2nd round of the League Cup at Highbury on 11th October 1967, Rod was again named as a sub.

Despite going a goal down in the 19th minute, Reading held their own for the first 45 minutes. When the second half started, the tempo and the game changed and Reading outfought Arsenal and even outclassed the Gunners.

Rod came on 15 minutes in the second half and 'worked tremendously hard in attack' and despite two headers by George Harris skimming the bar, a thunderous shot by Bayliss hitting the bar, and a goal disallowed for a foul on the Arsenal goalkeeper, Furnell, it was not enough and although Arsenal won the match 1-0, the night belonged to Reading for their tireless effort in running Arsenal ragged.

Roy Bentley was certainly pleased with the performance calling it *"The best performance by the team since I arrived at Elm Park"*

THE FOOTBALL LEAGUE CUP

SEASON 1967-68

FOOTBALL LEAGUE
CUP—Third Round

F.A. CUP WINNERS
1930, 1936, 1950

LEAGUE CHAMPIONS
1931, 1933, 1934, 1935,
1938, 1948, 1953

ARSENAL
v
READING

WEDNESDAY 11th October KICK-OFF 7.30 pm

ARSENAL STADIUM

Official Programme

3d

Arsenal   Reading

Colours:—Shirts: Red, White Sleeves.
Shorts: White.
Stockings: Blue and White Hoops.

Colours:—Shirts: Sky Blue.
Shorts: Sky Blue.
Stockings: Sky Blue.

Arsenal		Reading
FURNELL	1	WILKIE
STOREY	2	BAYLISS
McNAB	3	SPIERS
McLINTOCK	4	MELDRUM
NEILL	5	CHAPMAN
URE	6	YARD
RADFORD	7	FOSTER
SIMPSON	8	SCARROTT
GRAHAM	9	ALLEN
SAMMELS	10	SAINTY
ARMSTRONG	11	HARRIS
ADDISON	12	THORNHILL

Referee: Mr. K. E. WALKER (Maidstone, Kent)
Linesman: (Red Flag): C. F. ATTWELL (Northampton)
Linesman: (Yellow Flag): D. J. DARGAVEL (Grays, Essex)

READING 1967-68

(Photograph by courtesy of "Reading Evening Post")

Back row: R. Thornhill, D. Allen, E. Yard, A. Wilkie, P. Silvester, R. Bayliss, R. Spiers.
Front row: G. Harris, J. Mullen, C. Meldrum, R. Foster, J. Chapman.

Arsenal program front cover, team line ups and team picture on the back of the program

With centre-half and captain Colin Meldrum suspended for 14 days, Rod was brought into the side as cover for Meldrum for his first start of the season away to Bournemouth on 21st October. It was hoped that Rod could settle down into the position straight away, and despite two disallowed goals, Reading lost 2-0, with Rod giving away a penalty for a handball.

Rod was dropped down to the bench for the next game as an unused substitute before being dropped into the reserves until March.

Whilst playing consistently well for the reserves during this period, Rod would also help out with some football coaching for his local team Mortimer Garth in the village he now lived in, but he was never allowed to play for them at any time. He was introduced by a fellow teammate, Gordon Neate, who was a friend of the Mortimer chairman, John Dell.

Ex Mortimer player Norman Kernutt remembers that coaching sessions would be about fitness and individual development. Steve Dell, son of Chairman John Dell, remembers there would be an emphasis on set-pieces as well. Steve recalled that the training sessions grew from 10 players to 15/20 when Rod started to coach the team, and in the second season when Rod was coaching the team, they finished second in the league and gained promotion

Rod would go to watch any matches he could to cheer them on, he also had all the players around for New Year's party at his house in Campbell's Green in Mortimer.

Rod enjoyed doing the coaching, but it wasn't something he could commit too much time to as he was still working as a French polisher in the afternoon after training. Whilst a few other players had other jobs to supplement their income, for Rod, it wasn't all about money; he just enjoyed learning to become a French polisher as much as he enjoyed playing football professionally.

After missing 25 matches in the first team, including a 7-0 home defeat to Manchester City in an FA Cup round three replay, and after some good displays in the reserves, Rod finally got a recall to the team on 16th March 1967 for a home match against Bournemouth after the captain Colin Meldrum was ordered to rest by his doctor.

According to the local press, it was a surprise recall, but it was also acknowledged that Roy Bentley had looked to Rod before as "his ace in the pack."

Rod was a good choice for replacement for Meldrum and helped the team keep a clean sheet in a 1-0 win, with Reading hitting the woodwork three times and having two cleared off the line.

Roy Bentley had missed the Bournemouth game to go on a scouting mission, and with Colin Meldrum now fit again, he decided to drop Rod for the next game against Brighton, which was drawn 1-1. Rod remained on the bench for the next two games before another injury to Colin Meldrum saw Rod step into the side again.

Rod; looking to be fit for the Mansfield game

Reading fought out a well-deserved 2-2 against Mansfield, and with Meldrum still injured, Rod kept his place for the home match against Barrow on 12th April 1967.

Reading were sitting in 7th place in the league, only 6 points off a promotion place, and needed a good end-of-season run to push them into a promotion spot. With three games in four days, it was essential to get off to a good start.

A solid display against Barrow saw them run out 3-0 winners with Rod grabbing a headline of "Rod Thornhill star of tight defence" and the Reading Evening Post report went on to say that "Star of the team in this match was Rod Thornhill, with Docherty as the most dangerous forward."

There wasn't much time to take in the victory though as the very next day was another home match, this time with Watford the visitors and again, Reading put in another good display to win 2-0 with Rod again receiving the accolade of "star of defence" from the Evening Post.

The back-to-back wins had now taken Reading to within 3 points of a promotion spot, and with the return match away to Barrow, it was vital to get a good result two days later.

Rod and George Harris share a laugh on the coach to Barrow

Despite having 70% of the play, they slipped to an undeserved 1-0 defeat after missing too many chances. The Reading Evening Post reported "Bacuzzi, Chapman, Thornhill all gave little away and with Meldrum back after injury, the full back line gave a confident display." In fact, it was only one slip-up resulting in a goalmouth scramble which resulted in the Barrow goal.

The team stayed up north for the away game to Southport three days later. They trained on the beach and at Morecombe's ground in preparation for the game with the hope that despite the underserved loss to Barrow, they could carry on the good form to get back on the promotion trial, but it wasn't to be as Reading slipped to a 2-1 defeat to Southport.

There were always jokes and pranks going on when they travelled away, but it was at one away game up north. Rod cannot remember who they were playing at the time, that the team played a trick on the trainer, Jimmy Wallbanks.

The team was staying in a hotel, and as you walked up the stairs to the rooms, there was a large fish in a glass case perched on a shelf.

In the evening, after they had dinner, some of the players decided to take the fish down and put it in Jimmy's bed whilst he was down in the bar.

Rod was one of the four players involved in taking the fish down, whilst the other players kept Jimmy occupied in the bar. They got into Jimmy's hotel room, the bed was already made, so they turned back the covers, lifted the pillows, and slid the fish down into the bed. Jimmy was a bit annoyed when he realised there was a large fish in his bed, but he saw the funny side eventually. The hotel manager didn't see the funny side, though, and Reading FC were banned from using the hotel in the future!

Following the defeat to Southport, there followed a disappointing 1-0 home defeat to Oldham, which saw their promotion hopes dashed.

A section of the Elm Park crowd had not taken the Oldham result well and were calling for Roy Bentley to be sacked. They were throwing stones inside the ground, at the dressing room, on the ground and broke a corner flag! The Reading Evening Post commented that it was only a minority of supporters and told them "Come on, Kids, Grow up!"

Rod could always hear the crowd when he was playing, and he felt it was always a huge part of the game. On the whole, the crowd was encouraging with good comments and cheering, but Rod would occasionally get a bit of stick from some supporters, but as Rod says, you can't please everyone!

It was always in one area, in line with the penalty spot towards the Tilehurst End, where a small group would give Rod a rollicking, especially when he used to take a throw in that area, but Rod would just laugh it off. He says, looking back at it, you couldn't take notice of it and just took the good comments with the nasty comments. He remembers that all the players got stick at some point when they were playing, and some players would handle it better than others.

Rod remembers a young winger, Alan Scarrott, was taking stick from some parts of the crowd when he got into the team, and he was getting fed up with it and wanted to move. Roy Bentley was good at managing these situations though, and Scarrott stayed at the club for another two seasons.

The Evening Post was also calling for Bentley to stop switching between the 4-3-3 and 4-2-4 formations he was using and go back to a more orthodox WM formation that may produce better things in the future!

A much better performance resulted in a 2-1 home win over Scunthorpe Utd in the next game.

Before the next match, away to Oldham, Rod received the news that along with Ron Foster, Dennis Allen, and Ron Bayliss were to be placed on the transfer list and were now open to offers from other clubs. The news didn't affect Rod's game, though, and after a tight display from Rod and the defence, they gained their revenge on Oldham with an impressive 3-1 away win.

The season's final match saw them at home to Torquay Utd, who at one stage of the season had been top and still had an outside chance of going up if they could win, and other results went their way.

Torquay came out with all guns blazing in the first ten minutes of the game but couldn't convert any of their chances. Reading then settled down to playing neat, constructive football, scoring four goals with the defence, including Rod, keeping a clean sheet.

It must have been frustrating for the supporters and everyone at the club to see the team record three straight wins at the end of the season and finish just 5 points off a promotion place in 5th place.

It was a season of what could have been, and it meant that the club was to remain in the third division for the 37th successive season and to make matters worse, local rivals Oxford Utd were to finish top and gain promotion to the second division.

Rod made 13 appearances this season with 2 League Cup appearances and no goals scored.

1967-68 Division 3 Table

	Team	Pl	W	D	L	F	A	Pts
1	Oxford Utd (P)	46	22	13	11	69	47	57
2	Bury (P)	46	24	8	14	91	66	56
3	Shrewsbury Town	46	20	14	12	61	46	55
4	Torquay Utd	46	21	11	14	60	56	53
5	**READING**	**46**	**21**	**9**	**16**	**70**	**60**	**51**
6	Watford	46	21	8	17	74	50	50
7	Walsall	46	19	12	15	74	61	50
8	Barrow	46	21	8	17	65	54	50
9	Peterborough Utd	46	20	10	16	79	67	50
10	Swindon Town	46	16	17	13	74	51	49
11	Brighton	46	16	16	14	57	55	48
12	Gillingham	46	18	12	16	59	63	48
13	Bournemouth	46	16	15	15	56	51	47
14	Stockpot County	46	19	9	18	70	75	47
15	Southport	46	17	12	17	65	65	46
16	Bristol Rovers	46	17	9	20	72	78	43
17	Oldham Athletic	46	18	7	21	60	65	43
18	Northampton Town	46	14	13	19	58	72	41
19	Orient	46	12	17	17	46	72	41
20	Tranmere Rovers	46	14	12	20	62	74	40
21	Mansfield Town (R)	46	12	13	21	51	67	37
22	Grimsby Town (R)	46	14	9	23	52	69	37
23	Colchester Utd (R)	46	9	15	22	50	87	33
24	Scunthorpe Utd (R)	46	10	12	27	56	87	32

1966-67 Combination Division 2 Table

	Team	PL	W	D	L	F	A	Pts
1	Bristol City Reserves	40	22	9	9	89	56	53
2	Norwich City Reserves	40	23	5	12	77	60	51
3	Bristol Rovers Reserves	40	17	9	14	79	67	43
4	**READING RESERVES**	**40**	**18**	**5**	**17**	**64**	**61**	**41**
5	Swansea Town Reserves	40	15	10	15	81	65	40
6	Crystal Palace Reserves	40	16	8	16	67	71	40
7	Fulham Reserves	40	14	9	17	63	70	37
8	Cardiff City Reserves	40	14	9	17	60	69	37
9	Bournemouth Reserves	40	12	10	18	49	69	34
10	Oxford Utd Reserves	40	12	9	19	47	65	33
11	Brighton Reserves	40	12	5	22	54	77	31

READING
FOOTBALL CLUB - OFFICIAL PROGRAMME 6d

FOOTBALL LEAGUE DIV. III SATURDAY, 2nd SEPTEMBER, 1967

THE ORIENT

READING F.C. 1967/68

SEASON 1967/68

READING
FOOTBALL CLUB - OFFICIAL PROGRAMME 6d

FOOTBALL LEAGUE DIV. III SATURDAY, 16th MARCH, 1968

BOURNEMOUTH

SEASON 1967/68

Chapter 9: 1968-69 - Mr Reliability

READING 1968-69

Reading FC Team Photo – 1968-69 – Rod in the back row, second left.

In the summer of 1968, player/coach Jimmy Wheeler accepted the manager position at Fourth Division, Bradford City.

He was to take defender Ron Bayliss with him on his new venture, but he had also asked Rod if he would come up to Bradford to join him. Rod did think about it, but he felt settled at Reading, and he didn't want the upheaval of moving the family to Bradford, so he politely declined the offer, but it was a testament to Rod's reputation as a player that Jimmy Wheeler had asked him. Bradford finished fourth at the end of this season and gained promotion.

Reading had resumed training on 15th July 1968, with Rod still negotiating a new contract which was eventually extended on 16th November.

```
To : Mr. R. J. Romfuil
     10 Campbell Green
     the Avenue, Mortimer, Berks.

Dear Sir,          READING FOOTBALL CLUB LIMITED.
                     Notice of Exercise of Option.
          In exercise of the Option provided by Clause 17 (b) of
the Agreement made the.... 16th November,..... 196.5. between
the above Club and yourself, I, as Secretary acting with the
authority and on behalf of such Club now give you notice that the
Club hereby renews the said Agreement for a further period of
...... ONE YEAR, from the 30th day of June next.

          The remuneration, terms and conditions (excluding the
option provision contained in Clause 17 (b) of the present Agreement
between this Club and yourself) will continue to apply during the
further period.

          I shall be obliged if you will acknowledge receipt of
this letter by signing, dating and returning to me the printed form
at the foot of this letter, using the accompanying stamped addressed
envelope supplied herewith.

                                        Yours faithfully,

                                        Secretary-Manager,
                                        Reading Football Club.
```

After an excellent first-half display in a 1-1 draw with Brentford in a pre-season game, Rod was named as a substitute for the first game of the season against Stockport County on 10th August 1968. He was duly called upon in the 60th minute to replace Dick Spiers, who had hobbled off with a leg injury and played well as a replacement in a 2-2 draw.

As a result of his performance as a substitute, Rod was the automatic choice to replace Dick Spiers in the next game four days later for a visit to Colchester Utd in the first round of the League Cup. Reading went down to a disappointing 2-0 defeat, and were out of the cup at the first hurdle.

There wasn't much time to dwell on the defeat as Reading faced Northampton Town in the league at Elm Park just two days later. This time Roy Bentley was "delighted with the work rate" and he praised the players in a 1-0 win saying that "they ran and chased and gave me all the endeavour I could have asked for and it was good to hear the crowd appreciating it.

Roy Bentley called upon four first-teamers, including Rod, to strengthen the reserves for a fixture against Notts Forest Reserves before Rod was in action again for a visit to Plymouth in the league on 24th August.

Before the Plymouth game, Rod was presented with a testimonial cheque, having been at the club as a professional for 5 years, although he can't remember now what the amount was and what he spent the money on!

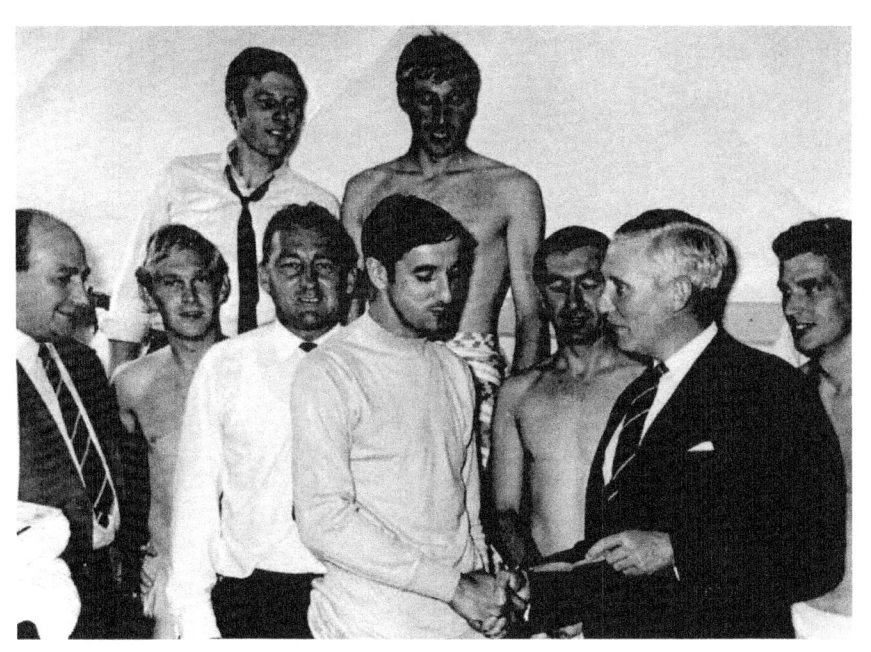

Rod is presented with a testimonial cheque from Chairman Frank Waller as the players, and Roy Bentley look on

Roy Bentley decided to switch to a 4-3-3 formation for this game, and in heatwave conditions, although losing 3-1, it had been a good performance up until the 68th minute, when a goalkeeping error and an own goal sealed Reading's fate on the day.

Rod moves in to help keeper Reading keeper Roy Brown, as the Plymouth forward moves in.

A spirited 0-0 draw in the next game away to Swindon then saw the visit of Hartlepool in the next game on 30th August with Bentley reverting to a 4-3-3 formation. The switch seemed to work well with a clean sheet for Rod and the defence, with Peter Silvester helping himself to 4 goals in an emphatic 7-0 win to round off the first month of the season in 4th place in the league, two points off a promotion place.

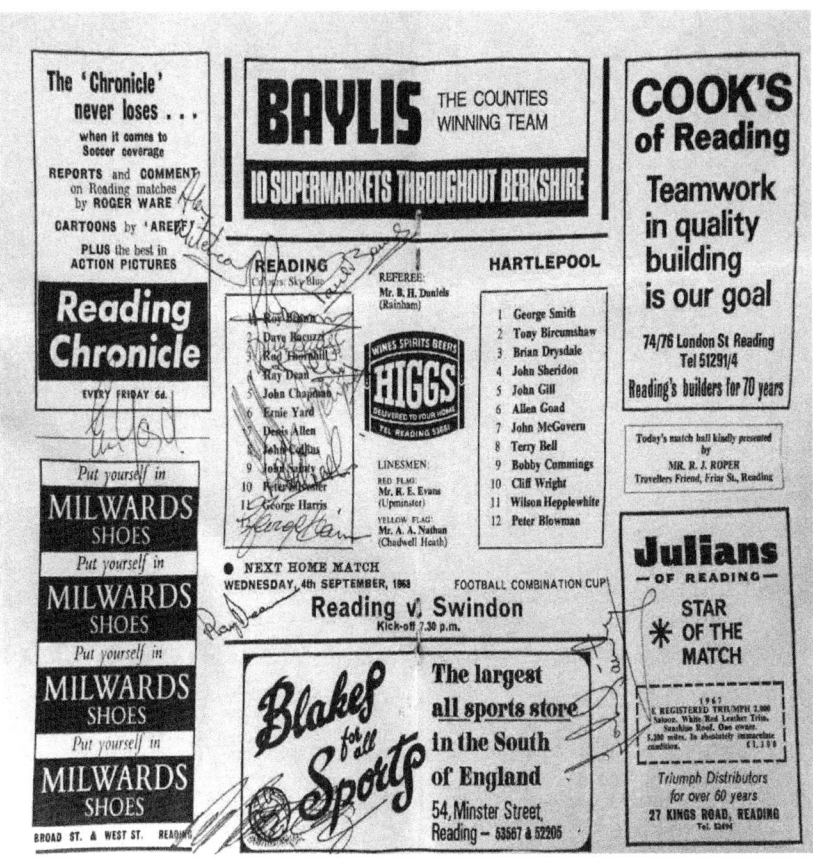

Signed program from the Reading v Hartlepool match

It was a disappointing start to September with defensive lapses resulting in a 2-2 draw with Walsall, and then despite hitting the bar against Watford in the first 10 minutes, they went down to a 1-0 defeat at home.

© Mirrorpix/Reach Licensing. Watford keeper, Mike Walker, goes up to clear from Reading's Denis Allen and Rod Thornhill

The team picked themselves up for the next game away to Crewe Alexandra, and despite a spirited display from ten-man Crewe, they recorded a 2-1 win.

An away trip to Shrewsbury Town saw Reading up against former player Maurice Evans who had taken over as coach at the club at the start of the season, and of course, this would be his first step on a road that would eventually take Maurice back to Reading as a manager in 1977.

Reading raced into a 3-1 lead, and with 10 minutes to go, it looked like the away win was theirs, but two late goals meant Reading had dropped a valuable point.

A week later, Reading got back to winning ways with a morale-boosting 2-1 win over Bristol Rovers, which saw the team in 5th place and still just two points off a promotion place.

A new face was joining the Biscuit Men at the start of October, with Hull City veteran Ray Henderson joining as player-coach to replace Jimmy Wheeler.

On the pitch, a last-minute 3-2 win over Gillingham lifted the team within 2 points of top spot and 1 point away from a promotion place. However, in the next game, littered with errors by the team, they lost 1-0 to Swindon after Rod had passed the ball back to the Reading keeper only for a Swindon forward to nip in and shoot towards goal. Rod got back to hook the ball away, but the referee had already given a goal.

Maybe this mistake caused Roy Bentley to drop Rod down to number 12 and an unused reserve for the next game away to Tranmere, which resulted in a 2-1 defeat.

Rod was on the bench for the next game at home to Brighton on 18th October 1968 and came on for the injured John Docherty at the start of the second half and earned a headline in the Evening Post of, "THORNHILL PUTS READING BACK ON THE WINNING TRAIL" with a headed goal in the 54th minute in a 1-0 win. The Sunday

Mirror reported that Rod had "revitalised" the Reading attack when he had come on.

Rod scores with a headed goal in the 1-0 win over Brighton

Rod returned to the starting line-up in a more attacking role for the next game against Barnsley, providing most of the thrust when Reading went forward and also going close with a header in the second half. But Reading's patchy form continued with a disappointing 1-0 defeat, and the team had now dropped to 11th in the table, but still only 4 points off a promotion place.

Rod started in a midfield role for the home match against Mansfield Town on 2nd November 1968, and after a dour first half, Reading came out the better of the two sides, going

1-0 up through John Collins. Mansfield equalised 5 minutes from time, but Reading were not finished yet, and from the restart, Collins grabbed the winner for Reading.

For the last six games, Reading had won one game and then lost the next game, and they must have been confident of breaking this pattern with the next match at home to Orient, who had not won away all season. However, Orient scored after 3 minutes, and too often, good opportunities were missed by Reading, and the patchy form continued with a 1-0 defeat.

The spell was broken in the next game away to Southport with a 1-1 draw before there was a welcome relief from league action with the first round of the FA Cup at home to Plymouth on 18th November. It was Rod and Player/Coach Ray Henderson who grabbed the headlines in a 1-0 win with the Evening Post running the headline "HENDERSON AND THORNHILL STAR IN READING'S FINE CUP VICTORY" Rod received top ratings from Bentley saying "He did an excellent job in defence and moved into several good scoring positions upfront. A fine display"

Predictably, Reading lost the next game away to Torquay Utd 1-0 before hammering bottom of the table, Oldham Athletic 4-1 at home to continue the patchy form in November with the 'versatile' Rod now moved into the back four. Reading were now in 10th place, but still in contention of a promotion place, 5 points adrift.

It was FA Cup round 2 time again on 7th December 1968 with a home tie against Torquay Utd in a match that Roy Bentley was calling vital to both sides.

For Reading, it would be to win back some public support after the patchy form in the league. The tie would go to a replay after a 0-0 draw at Elm Park with Torquay content to sit back and defend and Reading, unable to break them down. Roy Bentley's response to the draw was to cut training by 50% to give the players a rest.

It was not all doom and gloom, though, as Bentley pointed out that the players felt all along that they would have a better chance at Plain Moor as they believed Torquay would have to base their plans on the attack this time and leave Reading room to work on a defence, they felt they could exploit.

Although going 1-0 down before halftime, Reading came out the better team in the second half, taking the game to the home team and were rewarded with two goals to win the match and earn a plum tie in the next round, away to First Division, Newcastle Utd.

After back-to-back wins in the league and cup, there seemed to be new-found confidence in the team, and in icy conditions, Reading dominated in a 2-0 home win over Tranmere Rovers.

In the next game away to Brighton, it seemed things were continuing to go well for Reading, who were dominating the first half and should have gone into the break at least one up, but they were to pay the price for a penalty miss in the first half. Brighton scored two minutes into the second half, and Reading seemed to go pieces conceding another goal, two minutes from time.

With three days to go until the last game of 1968 against Gillingham on Boxing Day, a flu epidemic hit the club with Dave Bacuzzi, Paul Bence, and Rod sent home with flu-like symptoms.

Rod recovered enough to take his place in defence and, although lucky not to have been booked, performed "consistently well" during the game in a 2-2 draw to leave Reading in 8th place at the end of the year, 5 points away from a promotion place.

The first game of 1969 saw Reading visit, St James Park, for the third round FA Cup tie against Newcastle. With snow and ice covering the country, Roy Bentley ordered new rubber football boots for the players to try out during training at Elm Park, so they could feel comfortable, no matter what the conditions.

THREE MORE HEROES? — Rod Thornhill, Dennis Allan and Dick Spiers, of Reading, visit the cinema.

In Newcastle, some of the players, including Rod, went to a local cinema to relax and watch the western film' Shalako" the night before the game.

Reading started the game well and, for 20 minutes, threatened to take the lead as they took the game to Newcastle, pressing their defence. They were faster on the ball and more positive in their build-up than their 1st division opponents.

After 5 minutes of the game, Dennis Allen fired over, and three times, the Newcastle keeper was called into action to stop George Harris from scoring. The onslaught from Reading continued with the Newcastle keeper preventing Collins and Harris before Newcastle were able to break out while the Reading backline had pushed forward to beat the offside trap and score.

Within two minutes, another breakaway saw Newcastle go 2-0 up. Reading were not giving up, though and were unlucky not to get a goal back with John Collins striking the crossbar, and then George Harris was going close before half-time.

The backline of Bacuzzi, Spiers, Chapman, and Rod were all playing well, and they were not allowing the Newcastle forwards the chance to dictate the game.

The second half followed a familiar pattern with Reading carving out good chances but with no end result. Newcastle scored a third to kill off the game with ten minutes to go before adding a fourth, 3 minutes from time. It was a scoreline that did not portray how Reading had played against their first division opponents.

It was back to league duty on 11th January 1969 with a 1-1 draw away to Mansfield and then a goal 5 minutes from time gave Reading a 1-0 win over Southport, with Rod crowning a fine game by helping to keep a clean sheet for the team. He also sustained a gash to the leg after a challenge from a Southport player, which would prevent him from training leading up to the next game away to Orient.

Rod passed a fitness test to line up at centre-half for this game, and despite twice coming from behind, they were beaten 4-2 by Orient, who had been in the bottom 4 before the game.

Reading continued the inconsistent form in the next game with a well-deserved 3-2 win over Barnsley, and they were now 7 points off a promotion place.

Reading slipped to a 2-1 defeat at Luton on 1st February 1969 and were already 2-0 down when Dick Spiers was sent off. The sending off seemed to spur the ten men of Reading on, and despite getting a goal back, it wasn't enough to avoid defeat.

The news then came on 10th February 1969 that Roy Bentley had been sacked.

After informing Roy that his contract would not be renewed in November, it was agreed that he would leave the post straight away. Reading had been in Division 3 since 1931, and with promotion looking unlikely again this season with the team in 9th place and 10 points behind the leaders Watford, the board felt a change was necessary. Roy had worked tremendously hard to get Reading up into the Second Division, but he had been unable to achieve his goal in his 6 years with the club.

Player/Coach Ray Henderson was to take over team affairs whilst a new manager was found, and his first decision was to play all the first team in a reserve match against Swindon Reserves on 12th February to keep them sharp as the home match to Torquay on 8th February had been called off due to snow and freezing conditions.

When play was possible on 18th February, Reading travelled up to Oldham. Oldham were at the bottom of the league and Reading could only manage a 1-1 before there was another enforced rest on 22nd February due to a flooded pitch at Elm Park.

Conditions had improved for the home match against Stockport County on 28th February. Reading went 1-0 up in the 32nd minute after Rod, who was marking ex Everton and Scotland centre-forward Alex Young out of the game, placed a perfect pass to John Sainty, who rounded the keeper, and a deflection went straight to John Docherty to score an easy goal.

Stockport equalised before a second goal by Docherty shortly after halftime put Reading into a 2-0 lead. Two goals in two minutes from Harris and Sainty secured an impressive 4-2 win, with Stockport scoring a consolation goal in injury time.

READING F.C.
Division Three 1968-1969

Back Row: Roy Brown — Ernie Yard — Peter Silvester — Rod Thornhill — Colin Meldrum
Paul Bence   Dick Spiers
Front Row: George Harris — John Docherty — Dave Bacuzzi — John Chapman — John Santy

The Reading team that faced Stockport County on 28/2/69
– Rod sports a new moustache!

After the postponements due to bad weather, March was to be a busy time for the Biscuit Men with 9 matches scheduled, and it wasn't a good start on 4th March 1969.

Early pressure from home team, Rotherham, put Reading on the back foot. Still, Rod and his centre-half partner, Ray Dean, were coping well, and Rotherham were kept at bay until the last minute of the first half when Rotherham scored after Dave Bacuzzi conceded a free-kick. The second half started with Rotherham piling on the pressure resulting in two more goals. Silvester got one back for Reading before Rotherham scored again to round off a comprehensive 4-1 win.

Four days later, Reading were away to Northampton Town and took an early lead before the home team replied with 3 goals going into halftime. Reading came out a different team in the second half and took the game to Northampton reducing the deficit in the 57th minute. Reading continued to pile on the pressure, and Rod was unlucky not to equalise after a power header was saved at full length by the Northampton keeper who was keeping his side in the game. Reading continued to attack, and as they did so, Northampton took the opportunity to go up the other end to score a fourth and settle the match 4-2.

A 1-1 draw with Luton followed 4 days later before a disappointing 2-1 last minute home defeat to Plymouth followed by a certain referee, Mr Rex Spittle, ignoring claims for a certain penalty after John Sainty had been pulled down a few yards from the Plymouth goal.

Ray Henderson turned to Rod for more fire power upfront in the next game away to Barrow, playing him on the left-wing and although having a good game in this position, he wasn't able to influence the score line, the match finished 0-0.

Reading fell to another 2-0 defeat away to Hartlepool, although both Reading centre-halves were adamant that the ball had not crossed the goal line for the first goal.

There was a better end to March for Reading with a 1-0 home win over Rotherham followed by a 2-2 draw at home to Walsall, with Reading twice in front, and finally a 1-1 home draw with Torquay Utd.

It had been a poor March for Rod and the team, and with a record of 1 win, 4 draws, and 4 defeats, the team was now in 10th place in the league, 12 points away from promotion.

April was another busy month for Reading with 3 games in 4 days, starting at home to Bournemouth on 4th April.

After scoring in the first half, it looked like Reading were going to win 1-0, before Rod, who had moved back into defence for this game, was harshly judged to have pushed over a Bournemouth player in the penalty area 11 minutes from time. The Reading players were still arguing with the referee as Bournemouth converted the penalty to finish the game 1-1. Rod had argued too much, it seemed and was booked by the referee!

The following day, Reading travelled to Bristol Rovers and came away with a convincing and morale-boosting 3-1 win, and they followed this up just two days later with another 3-1 win at home to Crewe, and this earned the players a two-day break after the busy schedule. The good run had lifted the team to 9th place but still out of contention of a promotion place, 9 points behind.

The break, though, didn't seem to have worked as Reading returned to Elm Park four days later and this time, they suffered a 4-2 defeat in a disappointing performance against Shrewsbury Town.

Three days later, after 70 applicants had applied for the job, Jack Mansell was appointed the new Reading Manager, and he was to see his new side lose to a 1-0 scoreline in the next three games against Bournemouth, Watford, and Barrow.

© *Mirrorpix/Reach Licensing – the Spider is squeezed out by a cluster of Bournemouth defenders in the 1-0 defeat.*

Rod was an ever-present in the squad this season, appearing in every game bar one where he was named as the unused substitute. He made 45 league appearances, including 1 goal and 5 appearances in all cup competitions.

1968-69 Division 3 Table

	Team	Pl	W	D	L	F	A	Pts
1	Watford (P)	46	27	10	9	74	34	64
2	Swindon Town (P)	46	27	10	9	71	35	64
3	Luton Town	46	25	11	10	74	38	61
4	Bournemouth	46	21	9	16	60	45	51
5	Plymouth Argyle	46	17	15	14	53	49	49
6	Torquay Utd	46	18	12	16	54	46	48
7	Tranmere Rovers	46	19	10	17	70	68	48
8	Southport	46	17	13	16	71	64	47
9	Stockport County	46	16	14	16	67	68	46
10	Barnsley	46	16	14	16	58	63	46
11	Rotherham Utd	46	16	13	17	56	50	45
12	Brighton	46	16	13	17	72	65	45
13	Walsall	46	14	16	16	50	49	44
14	**READING**	**46**	**15**	**13**	**18**	**67**	**66**	**43**
15	Mansfield Town	46	16	11	19	58	62	43
16	Bristol Rovers	46	16	11	19	63	71	43
17	Shrewsbury Town	46	16	11	19	51	67	43
18	Orient	46	14	14	18	51	58	42
19	Barrow	46	17	8	21	56	75	42
20	Gillingham	46	13	15	18	54	63	41
21	Northampton Town (R)	46	14	12	20	54	61	40
22	Hartlepool (R)	46	10	19	17	40	70	39
23	Crewe Alexandra (R)	46	13	9	24	52	76	35
24	Oldham Athletic (R)	46	13	9	24	50	83	35

1968-69 Combination Division 1 Table

	Team	PL	W	D	L	F	A	Pts
1	Arsenal Reserves	25	20	4	1	71	18	44
2	Fulham Reserves	25	18	4	3	76	32	40
3	Tottenham Reserves	25	17	3	5	69	26	37
4	Ipswich Town Reserves	25	16	5	4	65	33	37
5	Crystal Palace Reserves	25	16	3	6	47	31	35
6	West Ham Reserves	25	9	13	3	42	28	31
7	Southampton Reserves	25	11	6	8	37	21	28
8	Gillingham Reserves	25	11	6	8	30	30	28
9	Bristol City Reserves	25	12	3	10	44	36	27
10	Walsall Reserves	25	9	6	10	41	38	24
11	Leicester City Reserves	25	9	6	10	35	37	24
12	Cardiff City Reserves	25	9	6	10	30	37	24
13	Peterborough Utd Reserves	25	7	10	8	32	36	24
14	QPR Reserves	25	8	7	10	39	45	23
15	Chelsea Reserves	25	9	4	12	43	43	22
16	Bristol Rovers Reserves	25	8	5	12	39	54	21
17	Bournemouth Reserves	25	6	9	10	33	46	21
18	Plymouth Argyle Reserves	25	6	9	10	23	37	21
19	Birmingham City Reserves	25	7	6	12	36	37	20
20	Norwich City Reserves	25	6	8	11	41	51	20
21	Swansea Town Reserves	25	7	6	12	38	49	20
22	Luton Reserves	25	5	10	11	28	51	20
23	Oxford Utd Reserves	25	7	4	14	26	52	18
24	Swindon Town Reserves	25	6	4	15	17	41	16
25	Northampton Town Reserves	25	5	3	17	27	59	13
26	**READING RESERVES**	25	4	4	17	24	65	12

READING

FOOTBALL CLUB - OFFICIAL PROGRAMME 9ᴰ
(INCORPORATING FOOTBALL LEAGUE REVIEW)

F.A. CUP 2nd ROUND SATURDAY, 7th DECEMBER, 1968

TORQUAY UNITED

SEASON 1968/69

Chapter 10: 1969-70 – Injuries and Transfer Lists

Reading FC Team Photo 1969-70 – Rod in the back row, second left.

As soon as the 1968-69 season had ended in April, and whilst players from other clubs were off on their holidays, Jack Mansell arranged a two-week training session at Bisham Abbey to get a good look at his squad.

Rod was placed on the transfer list at a figure of £5,000 along with Ernie Yard, and several other players were released, as Jack Mansell set about clearing the decks.

> **THE READING FOOTBALL CLUB LTD.**
> Founded 1871
> Members of the Football Association, Berks and Bucks Football Association, The Football League
> Football Combination, The South East Counties Football League
>
> President - A. E. Smith, Esq.
> DIRECTORS - Chairman - F. V. Waller, Esq.   Vice-Chairman - D. P. Baylis, Esq.
> W. T. D. Vincent, Esq.   L. Davies, Esq.
>
> Telephone and Telegrams
> READING 57878-9-0
>
> Registered Office:
> **ELM PARK, NORFOLK RD.,**
> **READING**
> RG3 2EF
>
> Team Manager
> R. T. F. Bentley
> Secretary-Manager
> F. May
>
> 21st May, 1969.
>
> Mr. R. D. Thornhill,
> 10, Campbells Green,
> The Avenue,
> Mortimer, Berks.
>
> Dear Sir,
>
> Further to the enclosed letter I beg to inform you that your name has been placed on the open to transfer list, at a fee of
> £...5,000......
>
> Yours faithfully,
>
> Secretary-Manager.

Rod remembers Mansell coming in, gathering everyone together, and then telling all the players that he would be bringing in his own players and a lot of them would be leaving. Rod believed Mansell knew a lot about football, though, and knew the style he wanted to play, which was why he tried to bring his own players to do this.

Jack Mansell was also quoted in the press as saying "*We haven't a first-team squad here. Nobody is sure of a place. Anyone who might have been the star last season, or played a lot of games, is no more an automatic first-team choice than anyone else.*"

However, Mansell would also recognise the importance of tradition, the blue and white hoop kit was back after an absence of four seasons.

Gone were the days where Rod would have to buy his own football boots from Blakes in Reading. The players now had access to the best boots in the business through a mail-order catalogue, which Rod still has in his possession.

Of course, the boots in the catalogue shown are black and white and none of the hundreds of colours you see these days!

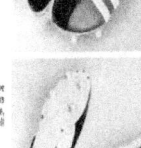

With 7 new signings, including the mercurial Tom Jenkins, who cost Reading £1,500 from Margate and was sold to Southampton for £60,000 in December 1969 after just 21 games played, Reading played their first pre-season game against Birmingham City. Rod was picked to play at centre-half in a 2-0 defeat with Rod going close to scoring with a header.

With just two days to go before the first game of the season, Rod finally put pen to paper and signed a one-year contract extension with a basic wage of £28 per week before incentives, which would work out at approximately £400 in 2021. A page of the contract below shows the financial incentives for that season.

Clause 15 Other Financial Provisions

a. The said player shall receive:
£n......... extra per week when playing in the first team.

b. £7....... per point in winning bonus in Football League fixtures up to and including a total of 46 points, to be paid monthly. The said player agrees to forego match bonuses as shown in Regulation 41.

c. A good start bonus shall be paid under the following conditions for the first six Football League matches played:-

    for 12 points gained £5 per point
    for 11 points gained £5 per point
    for 10 points gained £5 per point
    for 9 points gained £5 per point
    for 8 points gained £5 per point

d. £12.10s. 0d. per point in winning bonus in Football League fixtures to be paid for the 47th point up to and including the 56th point.

e. £25 per point in winning bonus in Football League fixtures for the 57th point onwards.

f. A special bonus as a once only payment of £8,000 shall be divided among the players appearing in Football League matches in proportion to their respective number of league appearances if the club obtains promotion from the third to second division. This payment to be made in the last week of the playing season.

F.A. Cup Competition

g. Round one match bonus as stated in Regulation 41.

    for appearing in round two   £10 per player
    for appearing in round three   £20 per player
    for appearing in round four   £45 per player
    for appearing in round five   £75 per player
    for appearing in round six   £110 per player
    for appearing in semi-final   £140 per player
    for appearing in the final   £200 per player
    Winners   £400 per player

h. £1 extra per week when the attendance exceeds 1,000 in the Football Combination Home matches.

10s. extra per week for each additional 500 in the Football Combination Home matches.

£5 extra per week when the Club occupies the first position in the Football Combination League Table.

£3 extra per week when the Club occupies the second position in the Football Combination League Table.

To be calculated from the Saturday evening League Table after the sixth Football Combination Fixture.

i. If a Player's registration be transferred at the request of the Club, and a fee obtained from the Transferee Club, 5% of such fee shall be paid, less income tax, to the player so transferred.

SIGNED AS A VERIFICATION OF ATTACHMENT TO AGREEMENT FORM

Player .... Secretary ....

Jack Mansell had seen enough of Rod in pre-season matches and training to hand him a place in the starting lineup at left-back in the first game of the season at home to Plymouth Argyle, and a 2-1 win gave them a good start to the season.

A solid display by both Rod and new signing Wilf Dixon kept the Gillingham wingers quiet in a 3-1 away victory in the next league match.

In between the first two league games of the season, Reading had drawn 1-1 with Colchester Utd in the League Cup, and with two wins and a draw in the first three games, hopes were high that in the replay at home, they could progress into the next round of the League Cup. The winners would have a money-spinning tie against first division Ipswich Town. However, it was disappointing performance from Reading which resulted in 3-0 loss to their lower league opponents, and they were out of the League Cup at the first hurdle.

The disappointment continued three days later in league with another home defeat, this time to Bristol Rovers in a 5-1 drubbing, which resulted in a slight knock during the game for Rod, which required treatment.

Having recovered in time for the Barnsley game three days later, Rod supplied a cross for Roger Smee to score one of the Reading goals in an exciting but disappointing, 4-3 away defeat.

The month of August ended with Rod having his best game of the season so far in a 0-0 away draw with Shrewsbury Town, with Dick Spiers returning to the side at centre-back. It had been a mixed start to the season, and the team was sitting in 12th place after games, 3 points off a promotion place.

On the 3rd September 1969, it was announced that with a staff of 27 professionals on the books, Reading were ready to unload some of the players, but still, Mansell refused to disclose any names. "We are overstaffed. We are aiming to get our numbers down to proportions that are economic"

September started well with a clean sheet for Rod and the defence in a 1-0 home win over Doncaster Rovers, and the defence was receiving good reports in the next game against Stockport County, despite conceding 2 goals in a 2-2 draw.

A 1-1 home draw with Torquay followed with Tom Jenkins showing off his skills in the match with his ball juggling, weaving, and beating a defender and then going back to beat the defender again!

In September, Reading continued their unbeaten record with a 2-0 home win against Bournemouth before being hit by illness and injury in the lead up to the next game away to Bury.

Rod was moved into midfield for this game and was unlucky not to get on the end of a Dixon cross in the first half, with the score at 0-0. The second half started with Bury scoring 2 goals in 5 minutes.

Reading pulled a goal back in the 68th minute after Dennis Allan had angled a pass for Rod to score his only goal of the season from close range, but it wasn't enough to avoid a 2-1 defeat.

The Chronicle reported that Rod, filling in for midfielder Bobby Williams, was one of the few players to emerge with any credit in this match.

Rod gets up to head away from a Bury cross

October saw Reading visit ex-player and Coach Jimmy Wheeler and his Bradford City side, who had been promoted from Division 4 and were unbeaten at home since December 1968.

It was an impressive record, and it stayed intact with a convincing 4-0 win over Reading, with Rod sustaining an injury to his back which would flare up again in training during the week.

Rod felt that he would not be fit for the next home match against Walsall and told Jack Mansell the day before the game. However, the next morning after a fitness test, he called Jack Mansell in the morning to say he was fit enough to play.

Rod had not been out of Reading's 12-man match day squad since 20th March 1968, playing 70 games, and on the other three occasions, he had been the substitute, so Rod was desperate to play to keep in the team.

Rod kept his place at left-back for the home match against Walsall in a 3-2 defeat though both Rod and Bobby Williams had shots cleared off the line. After the game, Colin Meldrum, a long servant of the club, put in a transfer request.

A fourth-minute goal at home to Gillingham on the 8th October 1969 saw Reading gain another two points; but, it was an eye injury after 60 minutes of the game, which would play an important part in the rest of Rod's career as a professional footballer.

Rod had to come off, and trainer Jimmy Wallbanks said after the game, "Rod could hardly see out of the eye last night. I think he damaged a small muscle. The club doctor said it wasn't too serious, but Rod was going for a hospital check-up if he thought it was necessary." The club doctor told Rod to rest for the next 5 days, which meant he missed the next game against Orient, which Reading won 1-0.

A week later, Rod was still on the sidelines and was told to rest another week. Rod said to the Reading Evening Post at the time "The eye hasn't been painful, just hazy, with a bit of blur. It all seems a bit silly, really. It didn't even go black when I got the knock, though the pupil is swollen. I've had a bit of internal bleeding, and it seems there are some cells floating around. The specialist told me that rest is the only thing for it. However, it is okay for watching TV and reading."

Rod – Told to Rest

Rod missed a 2-1 defeat away to Mansfield on 18th October 1969, and in the meantime, George Harris and Colin Meldrum had been sold to Cambridge Utd with John Sainty also putting in a transfer request during this time. Mansell was slowly getting rid of players from the Bentley era.

Rod was back in training leading up to the home match against Rotherham on 25th October with the eye apparently fully healed, and he was fit enough to regain his place in the team at left-back in place of Fred Sharpe with the game ending in a drab 1-1 draw.

Disappointed with the performance against Rotherham Utd, Jack Mansell arranged a friendly with Oxford University on 30th October, just two days before an away trip to Rochdale.

Mansell was looking for a good team performance with the threat of changes if there wasn't. The plan backfired with the first team losing 2-0 and Les Chappell requiring stitches for a foot injury, and Rod received an injury to his knee, causing swelling. Rod was ruled out for the trip to Rochdale just as he had got back into the team from his eye injury. The team lost 3-2 to Rochdale.

The knee healed well, and Rod was soon back in training and was picked to play left-back for the next game at home to Brighton, helping to keep a clean sheet in a 1-0 win.

After the exit in round 1 of the League Cup, it was hoped that Reading could have a better run in the FA Cup and with a tie against non-league Brentwood Town, they should have had a comfortable route into round 2, but another poor display by the team saw them humiliated 1-0 and dumped out of the FA Cup at the first hurdle.

Jack Mansell was looking for a good reaction to the cup exit and faced an away trip to Southport a week later. However, it was another disappointing result for Reading, who suffered a 6-2 thrashing with Rod at left-back and right back Wilf Dixon, both suffering a torrid time from the Southport wingers. The team was now just 4 points off a relegation place.

Rod's injury-prone season continued arriving back from the Southport match with a leg injury which was to keep him out of the side for the next three games before being back in contention for a place in the team for the trip to Doncaster on 20th December 1969. However, it was not to be with the game called off due to heavy overnight snow, and this also ended Rod's involvement with the first team for the rest of the season.

Rod returned to the reserves on 10th January 1970, playing in an attacking position in a 4-0 defeat to Southampton.

There was an occasional benefit to playing in the reserves, though, in that some of the bigger teams would play first teamers in their reserves, and Rod was up against Frank Lampard (senior) and John Charles in a 2-0 cup win over West Ham Reserves on 28th January.

The next reserve game would be at home to Southampton Reserves on 4th February 1970, and this would be Rod's last ever game in the colours of Reading in a 1-1 draw.

Rod's eye was clearly not right. After being recommended to attend the hospital, it was found that Rod had suffered a detached retina in the game against Gillingham on 8th October 1970 and was told to rest the eye completely.

```
THE READING FOOTBALL CLUB LIMITED
Registered Office: Elm Park, Norfolk Road, Reading

FOOTBALL COMBINATION
READING v. SOUTHAMPTON
WEDNESDAY, 4th FEBRUARY 1970
at 7.30 p.m.
```

READING Blue and White Hoops		SOUTHAMPTON Red and White	
1	J. Pratt	1	G. Gurr
2	D. Bacuzzi	2	R. McCarthy
3	D. Butler	3	D. Hollywood
4	D. Spiers	4	F. Kemp
5	T. Ryan	5	J. McGrath
6	S. Morgan	6	R. Fry
7	J. Docherty	7	D. Thompson
8	R. Thornhill	8	F. Saul
9	R. Smee	9	A. Simpson
10	M. Swain	10	D. MacLeod
11	J. Harley	11	J. Sydenham
12		12	L. Harfield

REFEREE:
Mr. T. D. Spencer
(Church Crookham)

LINESMEN:
Red Flag:
Mr. D. R. O'Neill (Swindon)
Yellow Flag:
Mr. J. W. Eden (Oxford)

★ *ELM PARK ATTRACTION* ★

Saturday next, 7th February   FOOTBALL LEAGUE   Kick-off 3 p.m.

ORIENT

PROGRAMME: PRICE 2d.

Program from Rod's last game for Reading Reserves

Rod would receive the all-clear from his eye specialist to resume playing in May 1970, but by this time, the club had given Rod a free transfer, and he was free to look for a new club.

Rod had made 16 appearances in the league in his final season, scoring once, and he made 3 appearances in all cup competitions.

Rod had finished his career with Reading making 221 appearances in all competitions and scoring a total of 23 goals. Not bad for a home-grown lad from Reading!

The first team finished the season in 8th place in the league, 7 points from promotion.

The following season, there would be no players left from the Roy Bentley era for Reading. They would finish the season 4th from bottom and relegate to Division 4, with Jack Mansell sacked as manager after a poor run of results at the start of the 1971/72 campaign.

1969-70 Division 3 Table

	Team	Pl	W	D	L	F	A	Pts
1	Orient (P)	46	25	12	9	67	36	62
2	Luton Town (P)	46	23	14	9	77	43	60
3	Bristol Rovers	46	20	16	10	80	59	56
4	Fulham	46	20	15	11	81	55	55
5	Brighton	46	23	9	14	57	43	55
6	Mansfield Town	46	21	11	14	70	49	53
7	Barnsley	46	19	15	12	68	59	53
8	**READING**	46	21	11	14	87	77	53
9	Rochdale	46	18	10	18	69	60	46
10	Bradford City	46	17	12	17	57	50	46
11	Doncaster Rovers	46	17	12	17	52	54	46
12	Walsall	46	17	12	17	54	67	46
13	Torquay Utd	46	14	17	15	62	59	45
14	Rotherham Utd	46	15	14	17	62	54	44
15	Shrewsbury Town	46	13	18	15	62	67	44
16	Tranmere Rovers	46	14	16	16	56	59	44
17	Plymouth Argyle	46	16	11	19	56	54	43
18	Halifax Town	46	14	15	17	47	63	43
19	Bury	46	15	11	20	75	72	41
20	Gillingham	46	13	13	20	52	74	39
21	Bournemouth (R)	46	12	15	19	48	71	39
22	Southport (R)	46	14	10	22	48	66	38
23	Barrow (R)	46	8	14	24	46	81	30
24	Stockport County (R)	46	6	11	29	27	71	23

1969-70 Combination Division 1 Table

	Team	PL	W	D	L	F	A	Pts
1	Arsenal Reserves	25	18	5	2	68	25	41
2	Tottenham Reserves	25	15	8	2	49	16	38
3	Ipswich Town Reserves	25	16	2	7	61	23	34
4	Birmingham City Reserves	25	13	8	4	61	26	34
5	Bristol City Reserves	25	15	4	6	43	30	34
6	West Ham Reserves	25	14	5	6	51	31	33
7	Cardiff City Reserves	25	11	9	5	38	27	31
8	Leicester City Reserves	25	13	4	8	51	34	30
9	Crystal Palace Reserves	25	11	7	7	43	30	29
10	Plymouth Argyle Reserves	25	12	5	8	37	32	29
11	Swansea City Reserves	25	10	8	7	27	21	28
12	Oxford Utd Reserves	25	11	5	9	41	36	27
13	Luton Town Reserves	25	11	5	9	44	42	27
14	Norwich City Reserves	25	8	8	9	29	28	24
15	**READING RESERVES**	**25**	**7**	**9**	**9**	**31**	**44**	**23**
16	Bournemouth Reserves	25	7	8	10	37	42	22
17	Swindon Reserves	25	9	4	12	32	41	22
18	Southampton Reserves	25	8	5	12	41	50	21
19	Chelsea Reserves	25	8	4	12	37	43	20
20	Fulham Reserves	25	6	7	12	32	36	19
21	QPR Reserves	25	7	5	13	38	47	19
22	Bristol Rovers Reserves	25	7	2	16	31	62	16
23	Gillingham Reserves	25	4	6	15	21	60	14
24	Walsall Reserves	25	3	7	14	16	44	13
25	Northampton Town	25	3	4	18	19	62	10
26	Peterborough United	25	3	4	18	15	63	10

Reading Football Club

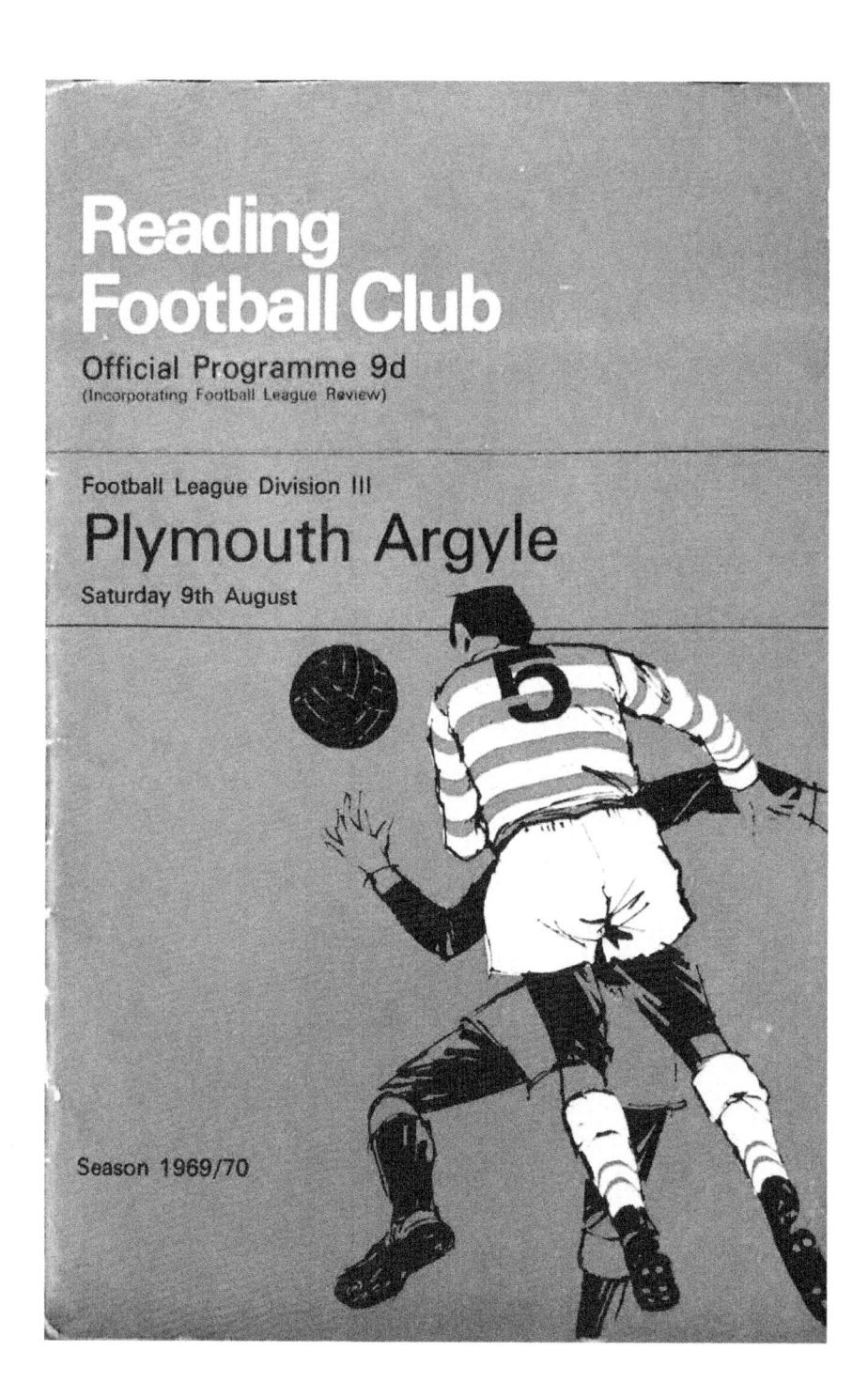

Official Programme 9d
(Incorporating Football League Review)

Football League Division III
Plymouth Argyle
Saturday 9th August

Season 1969/70

Chapter 11: 1970-71 – The Dolphins Of Poole

Poole Town Team Photo FC 1970/71 – Rod in the back row, far left.

After being released by Reading in May 1970, Rod had received offers from league club Scunthorpe Utd and non-league Poole Town. Rod and Janet were not keen to move the family up north, so after a phone call from the Poole Town chairman, Rod and Janet made their way to Poole Town Stadium on Wimborne Road, and while Janet took the kids to Poole Park, Rod took a look around the Stadium. He was impressed with the facilities and how the club was run.

It was an easy choice to make to move to the beautiful town of Poole on the south coast to carry on playing competitively on a part-time basis, and there was also another addition to the family with their third son, Ian, the author, born on 1st June 1970.

Poole Town, nicknamed The Dolphins, played in the Southern Premier League and were managed by Tom McInnes. The team had been promoted from the Southern Division 1 in the 1964/65 season and then had struggled at the lower end of the Premier League table ever since, finishing in 18th place out of 22 teams in the 1969/70 season.

There had been records of a "Kinde of Football" being played in Poole as long ago as 1649, the year of King Charles 1st execution and club records for the year the club was founded in 1880, show listed under expenditure, a fee to keep the pitch free from seaweed as the pitch was so close to the sea!

The stadium was impressive for a non-league side with a seated stand that could seat between 1500 – 2000 spectators and up to date floodlighting, all part-funded by the Poole supporters club, which at that time had an incredible 35,000 members.

The football team shared the facilities with Greyhound racing and the Poole Pirates speedway team with the football pitch sitting inside the greyhound track and speedway track, meaning supporters were sat quite a way back from the action, which was said to affect the atmosphere sometimes.

Rod's contract remained the same in the two seasons he was at the club on a basic wage of £16 per week in the close season and £20 a week when the season started with bonuses for appearances and league position at the end of the season.

P

An Agreement made the NINTH

day of MAY 19 71 between NORMAN A BAILEY of THE STADIUM POOLE in the County of DORSET the Secretary of and acting pursuant to Resolution and Authority for and on behalf of the POOLE TOWN FOOTBALL CLUB of THE STADIUM POOLE (hereinafter referred to as the Club) of the one part and RODNEY DEREK THORNHILL of 10 CAMPBELLS GREEN MORTIMER NR READING in the County of BERKSHIRE Professional Football Player (hereinafter referred to as the Player) of the other part **Whereby** it is agreed as follows:—

1. The Player hereby agrees to play in an efficient manner and to the best of his ability for the Club for the period of ONE (year/years) (hereinafter called "the initial period of employment") from the NINTH day of MAY 1971 to the First Saturday in May 1972 or the last day of the playing Season as determined by the League of which the Club is a member, whichever is the later unless the initial period of employment shall either be (a) previously determined in accordance with the provisions of one or other of Clauses 10, 11 or 12 hereof or (b) terminated extended or renewed as provided by Clauses 17 and 18 of this Agreement.

2. The Player shall attend the Club's ground or any other place decided upon by the Club for the purposes of or in connection with his training as a Player pursuant to the instructions of the Secretary, Manager, or Trainer of the Club, or of such other person, or persons as the Club may appoint.

3. The Player shall do everything necessary to get and keep himself in the best possible condition so as to render the most efficient service to the Club, and will carry out all the training and other instructions of the Club through its representative officials.

4. The Player shall observe and be subject to all the Rules, Regulations and Bye-Laws of The Football Association, and any other Association, League, or Combination of which the Club shall be a member. And this Agreement shall be subject to any action which shall be taken by The Football Association under their Rules for the suspension or termination of the Football Season, and if any such suspension or termination shall be decided upon the payment of wages shall likewise be suspended or terminated, as the case may be and in any proceedings by the Player against the Club it shall be a sufficient and complete defence and answer by and on the part of the Club that such suspension or termination hereof is due to the action of The Football Association, or any Sub-Committee thereof to whom the power may be delegated.

5. The Player shall not engage in any business or live in any place which the Directors (or Committee) of the Club may deem unsuitable.

6. Unless this Agreement has previously been determined by any one of Clauses 10, 11 or 12 hereof as hereinafter provided, the Player shall not before the last day of the playing season next preceding the expiration of any further or additional further period for which this Agreement shall have been renewed in accordance with the provisions of Clauses 17 or 18 hereof or before the last day of the playing

13. The following special provisions laid down by the Competitions in which the Player will compete are accepted by and will be observed by the Player:—

14. Basic Wages.

£ 16 per week from 9th MAY 1971 to 14th AUGUST 1971
£ 20 per week from 14th AUGUST 1971 to 6th MAY 1972
£ ...... per week from ...... to ......
£ ...... per week from ...... to ......
£ ...... per week from ...... to ......
£ ...... per week from ...... to ......
£ ...... per week from ...... to ......
£ ...... per week from ...... to ......

15. Other financial provisions:—
(Fill in as required).

a) The Player to be paid an extra £2 per week when appearing in the First Team.

b) The Player to participate in League Position Bonus at end of season as follows:—

Share of £800 as Premier Div Southern League Champions
 " " £700 "   "   "   "   "   "   Runners-up
 " " £600 for 3rd Place
 " " £500 " 4th   "
 " " £300 " 5th   "
 " " £250 " 6th   "
 " " £200 " 7th   "
 " " £150 " 8th   "
 " " £100 " 9th   "
 " " £50   " 10th "

c) Match Bonus — As per Rule.

Poole's policy at the time seemed to be on the side of recruiting older players from the football league with good experience. Rod obviously had 7 years playing professionally for Reading, but also in the Poole ranks at the time were Phil Ferns, an ex-Liverpool player who had played enough games in the 1963/64 season to earn a championship medal, Irving Brown, who had played for Brighton and Bournemouth, Rod Taylor, who had league experience with Portsmouth, Gillingham and Bournemouth, Dennis Pring, who had played for Southampton, Ray Keeley, who had played for Mansfield Town, Ken Hodgson had played for Newcastle, Scunthorpe, Bournemouth and Colchester, John Brewster had played for Sheffield Utd, Peter Arrowsmith had been at Southampton and Torquay Utd, Steve Pegram had been at Notts Forest and goalkeeper Alan Buck, had played for Colchester Utd.

It was undoubtedly a side bursting with experience, and for Rod, he would be switching from the blue and white hoops of Reading to the Red and White hoops of Poole at the time.

Rod and Janet started the season still living in Mortimer in Reading, and Rod would travel down to training once a week and then play matches on Saturday, whilst Janet would take the kids to Poole Park when he played at home.

Rod took on a new role at the start of his Poole career, playing as a sweeper behind the back four. Rod remembers his role as a sweeper and explained that he would line up in front of the back four in the half-back line, but then he had to adjust his position when the other team was attacking, so he could then drop to be behind the back four. He explains that you couldn't just stay behind the defence all the time as the opposition forward would just follow you and keep onside, so you had to always be thinking for yourself as to when you should get behind your defence to provide the cover. Rod enjoyed having that authority to make his own decisions on his positioning during the game, and he felt he had the energy and fitness to do so.

Even though he was playing as a sweeper, he was still able to get forward on occasions, and he opened his scoring in only his second appearance for the club on 18th August 1970 after finishing off a good set piece. Unfortunately, it wasn't enough to avoid a 3-2 home defeat to Bath City.

Rod celebrates his goal against Bath City.

Two games later, they were up against a strong Cambridge City side and drew 1-1, but it was Rod who missed the best chance for Poole in the second half.

In the next game against league leaders, Chelmsford City, Rod, again, had a good opportunity to score after his header had beaten the Chelmsford keeper, but the ball hit the post and the game finished 0-0.

On 14th November 1970, Rod arrived late for the league match away to Telford Utd. Poole were already down to just eleven healthy players due to an injury crisis and had to start with 10 men. After going a goal down within a minute of the start of the match, Rod arrived 5 minutes into the first half and put Poole up to full strength, but it wasn't enough to stop Telford from beating Poole 4-3.

Although the league form had been disappointing as 1970 drew to a close, with the team sitting in 18th place, just one place above the relegation zone, Poole were faring better in the cup competitions.

In the FA Cup preliminary round in September, Poole beat Chippenham Town 4-0 to enter the FA Cup qualifying rounds. The Daily Echo reported on the game that "the best display came from Rod Thornhill whose constant attempts to link defence and attack was never far short of a complete success."

There were still four matches to go before the chance to play a Division 3 or 4 sides from the Football League, and the first round in the qualifying round saw Poole beat Devizes with a comprehensive 5-1 win, with Rod scoring one of the goals with a shot 25 yards out. The next round saw Poole face another away trip to Salisbury, and they came away with a 1-0 win.

Before Poole were to meet Bath City in the third qualifying round of the FA Cup, there was the small matter of a second leg of the Western Counties Floodlight cup final for the 1969/70 season. Due to fixture congestion, the final had to be carried over into the 1970/71 season, and the first leg resulted in a comfortable 3-0 home win for Poole over Weymouth on 6th October 1970.

The second leg was played at Weymouth on 21st October 1970, and Poole went one up and increased their aggregate score to 4-0 with a goal in the 27th minute by Irving Brown. Weymouth came out fighting after the interval and had a couple of near misses with Irving Brown and Rod, blocking shots before they scored from a free-kick. But Poole increased the lead to 2-1 with a penalty in the 76th minute converted by Kenny Hodgson to win the match 2-1 and win 5-1 on aggregate to lift Poole's first trophy since the 1954/55 season.

Poole show off the Western Counties Floodlight Cup (Rod not in picture)

Three days later, it was round 3 of qualifying for the FA Cup with a home tie against Bath City, who were 8 places above Poole at the time in the Southern League, but a dominant Poole ran out winners with a well-deserved 1-0 win.

Poole were now just 90 minutes away from going into the draw for the first-round proper of the FA Cup, but it was always going to be a difficult match at home to Yeovil Town, who were sitting 5th in the table at the time. Despite outplaying Yeovil for most of the match, Poole were not able to convert their good chances, including a missed open goal, and Yeovil ran out the eventual winners with a 3-1 victory.

It was a similar story in the Southern League Cup with a 1-1 draw against Barry Town followed by a 1-0 win at home in the first round. Poole received a bye in the second round before another 1-1 draw was followed by a 1-0 win over Cheltenham Town.

Poole were now in the quarter-finals of the Southern League Cup for the first time in their history, but they would go no further with a 3-1 defeat to Telford Utd ending their cup run.

Back in the league, Poole had started 1971 in fine style with a double over Bedford Town. A 1-0 away win was followed by a 3-1 home win, with Rod described as 'cool and efficient under pressure' in the away win.

A 3-1 win over Dartford at the start of February lifted the team 6 points away from the relegation zone in a game where Rod was described as the star of the match.

The Dartford keeper punches away despite being challenged by Rod.

Poole only managed to gain 1 point in the next 5 games, which was a result of a 0-0 draw with Barnet, but only after Rod had saved the day by sprinting back to clear off the line after a Barnet player had lobbed the Poole keeper.

With the team just one point off the relegation zone at the beginning of March, manager Tom McInnes was released by the club, and it was left to coach, Jackie Fisher, to take the reins for the remainder of the season whilst the directors looked for a player-manager to take over.

Although Poole had finished near the bottom in previous seasons in the Southern Premier League, there was talk before the end of the season that the Football League and FA were to meet in April. Two of the recommendations included 12 non-league sides admitted into the Football League for the following season, with 8 expected to come from the Southern League. It was hoped that with Poole's stadium, good finances and the support the club could achieve, with 35,000 members of the supporter's club, that the Football League would invite Poole Town to take one the places. Unfortunately, this never came to fruition.

Poole finished the season with six consecutive home wins, including a 2-0 win over high flying Hereford in the last game of the season, with a certain "gentle giant" John Charles playing for Hereford. They were to finish 18th at the end of the season, 5 points away from the relegation zone.

Programme for the Hereford match

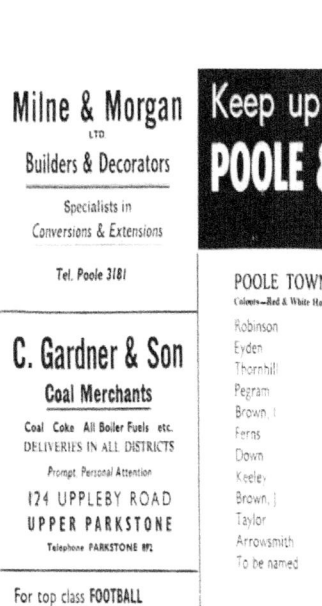

Despite Poole releasing six experienced players at the end of the season, Rod was on the retained list for next season.

Rod had made 42 appearances for the team and had scored 1 goal in the league and 1 goal in the cup.

1970-71 - Southern Premier League

	Team	Pl	W	D	L	F	A	Pts
1	Yeovil Town	42	25	7	10	66	31	57
2	Cambridge City	42	22	11	9	67	38	55
3	Romford	42	23	9	10	63	42	55
4	Hereford Utd	42	23	8	11	71	53	54
5	Chelmsford City	42	20	11	11	61	32	51
6	Barnet	42	18	14	10	69	49	50
7	Bedford Town	42	20	10	12	62	46	50
8	Wimbledon	42	20	8	14	72	54	48
9	Worcester City	42	20	8	14	61	46	48
10	Weymouth	42	14	16	12	64	48	44
11	Dartford	42	15	12	15	53	51	42
12	Dover	42	16	9	17	64	63	41
13	Margate	42	15	10	17	64	70	40
14	Hillingdon Borough	42	17	6	19	61	68	40
15	Bath City	42	13	12	17	48	68	38
16	Nuneaton Borough	42	12	12	18	43	66	36
17	Telford Utd	42	13	8	21	64	70	34
18	**POOLE TOWN**	**42**	**14**	**6**	**22**	**57**	**75**	**34**
19	Kings Lynn (R)	42	11	7	24	44	67	29
20	Ashford Town (R)	42	8	13	21	52	86	29
21	Kettering Town (R)	42	8	11	23	48	84	27
22	Gloucester City (R)	42	6	10	29	34	81	22

POOLE TOWN F.C.

v

WIMBLEDON

Southern League Premier Div.   Kick-off 3.0 p.m.

Saturday, 10th April, 1971

2½p

LUCKY NUMBER

This Programme is Published by The Supporters' Club.
Printed by The Ashley Press, Balena Close, Creekmoor Trading Estate, Poole. Tel. Broadstone 5656

FOR REPORTS OF TODAY'S MATCHES AND CLUB NOTES READ TONIGHT'S... SPORTS ECHO *On sale at all Newsagents*

Chapter 12 1971-72 – The Final Countdown

Poole Town Team Photo 1971-72 – Rod on back row second from left.

Rod, Janet and the family moved down to Dorset in the summer of 1971, selling their house in Mortimer and purchasing a new built 3 bedroomed house for £6,000 in West Way, Broadstone, four miles away from Poole. Although slightly inland from the coast, you could still see the sea and Old Harry Rocks in the distance.

Rod was able to continue playing football for Poole Town as well as having a milk round in the morning around the streets of Broadstone working for Unigate. He was also still able to ply a trade as a French polisher, working in the garage of the house at West Way, with work coming in from an advert in the yellow pages. Janet also had a job working at Plessey's in Poole on a part-time basis.

Janet remembers going to see a nativity play for their daughter Jane at her school one evening, and in front of them, they overheard two women gossiping about the local milkman who would always stop at 119 West Way and would be in there for half an hour! Janet had to tell them it was her husband and that's where they lived!

Before the 1970/71 season had ended, Poole were already looking for a player/manager to take over the reins from caretaker manager Jackie Fisher.

An advert had gone out in the Sunday People on 14th March 1971:

- **WANTED by Poole Town immediately – a player-manager. Wages and prospects are good.**

By the start of the 1971-72 season, Rod and the rest of the team had a new man in charge, with Tony Knapp taking over as player-manager on 1st July 1971 after the club had received 23 applications.

Tony Knapp had played for England B, Leicester City, Coventry City, Los Angeles Wolves, Tranmere Rovers and Southampton, where he had made 233 appearances, so he came with good experience.

One of Tony Knapp's first decisions was to change from the red and white hoops with white shorts to yellow shirts and blue shorts.

The pre-season started well for Poole with a morale-boosting 4-2 win over a strong Southampton side, with Rod scoring the second goal for Poole just before halftime.

Poole also made a good start to the season against newly-promoted Gravesend and Northfleet with Tony Knapp's tactics to "play it tight to look at the opposition and not give away an early goal", resulting in a 1-0 away win.

At the end of August, Rod suffered another injury to his eye in a 3-1 away defeat to Worcester City. The injury resulted in a trip to the hospital, where he received six stitches. But he was back just 3 days later playing in a 1-0 home win against Nuneaton Borough, although manager Tony Knapp admitted he shouldn't have really been out there!

In September, it was looking like Rod would be reacquainted with a couple of his ex-Reading teammates. It was reported that transfer fees had been agreed with Portsmouth FC for Ron Tindall and Mick Travers to join Poole, which would have provided the team with some much-needed firepower upfront. However, it wasn't to be, as both players were to turn down the move to Poole.

Rod, in his final season at Poole.

The team again lingered towards the bottom half of the league table all season, but this time, it was a disappointing cup campaign after only just failing at the final hurdle the previous season.

After winning the preliminary round in the FA Cup, 2-1 away to Minehead thanks to a 61st-minute winner from Rod who squeezed in a shot that the Minehead keeper could only paw over the line. They next faced lower league opposition Glastonbury in Round 1. Glastonbury were playing in the Western League at the time and had just been beaten 5-3 by Minehead in a league fixture a week before the cup game with Poole.

But it would be the lower league opposition who would go through to round 2 with a 2-1 shock win over Poole, despite good chances for Brown, Keeley and Rod in the second half to score for Poole. It was an 85th-minute goal for Glastonbury which put them through with their local newspaper headlining with the following.

"GLASTONBURY SHAKE STAR-STUDDED POOLE TOWN ELEVEN"

Shortly after this result, Poole were dumped out of the Southern League Cup in the first round by Guildford City, 3-2 on aggregate.

Rod was back to his sweeper duties against Folkestone on 25th September 1971 in a 0-0 draw, which included Rod's ex-teammate, Pat Terry, in the Folkestone lineup, who was kept quiet by the Poole defence.

Rod was to come up against quite a few of his Reading ex-teammates whilst playing for Poole. Ron Bayliss was playing for Yeovil Town; Johnny Petts was player-manager at Bath City, Colin Meldrum (player-manager), Dennis Butler, and Mick Fairchild were all playing for Hillingdon Borough.

It was against Hillingdon Borough on 13th November 1971 where Poole produced their brightest display of the season in a 3-1 home win with Rod playing at left-back. Rod not only starred in defence, but he also made several shrewd runs down the left. The result lifted the team to 13th in the league.

A home league match against Margate on 5th February 1972 saw an 11th-hour alteration to the playing area. With improvements to the speedway track around the pitch, five yards were lopped from each side of the pitch, causing the players to run out of space too many times. Poole lost the game 2-1.

Rod was called to appear before an FA disciplinary committee at the beginning of March 72 due to three bookings in a year. Rod can't remember appearing before the committee, but he does remember receiving a fine from the FA. In later life, whilst waiting in the Royal Berkshire Hospital in Reading for an operation for a replacement knee, the author asked him whether he could have asked the PFA for any assistance, and he replied, "I don't think so as I had a fine from the FA in my Poole days which I don't think I ever paid!"

After a poor run of results throughout March, Poole was sitting third from the bottom and 4 points from safety.

There was a much needed 3-2 win over Bath at the start of April, and Rod's header in the 73rd minute was going goal bound before being helped on its way by Poole's John Brown on the line to give Poole some hope in their battle against relegation.

It wasn't to be, though, as the final 6 games resulted in 3 draws and 3 losses and Poole were to finish 4th from bottom in 19th place at the end of the season, which would usually have meant relegation to Division 1, but this season they would be given a lifeline.

At that time, there was no automatic promotion and relegation from the non-league into the Football League, so a club would have to apply to the league to get promoted, and the application would then be considered. After the 1971/72 season had ended, Hereford Utd, were elevated into the Football League after finishing second in the Southern Premier League. This meant that Poole were able to stay up to help keep the numbers right in the league.

Hereford went on to finish 2nd in Division 4 of the Football League in the following season and gain promotion at the first attempt, which maybe shows the strength of the Southern Premier League at the time.

It was clear, though, at the end of the season, that the club would be looking to make changes. Although it had been reported in the Daily Echo in April 1972, before the season had ended, that Rod was on the retained list for the next season, this changed when Tony Knapp was replaced with Sid Miles after only one season in charge. There was a change in the club policy of buying older players from the football league, and they were also to implement a new wage structure.

They would now look to develop a younger side meaning there would be a complete overhaul of playing staff with only 6 players retained from the current squad for next season. Rod was one of the released players, so it was time to hang up his boots and retire from football and concentrate on his French polishing business.

Rod completed his final season with Poole with 40 appearances and 1 goal in the cup.

He had enjoyed two seasons at Poole, playing in a variety of positions as he had done at Reading throughout his career. He played left left-back, centre half, sweeper, left midfield and right midfield for Poole.

1971-72 - Southern Premier League

	Team	Pl	W	D	L	F	A	Pts
1	Chelmsford City	42	28	6	8	109	46	62
2	Hereford Utd (P)	42	24	12	6	68	30	60
3	Dover	42	20	11	11	67	45	51
4	Barnet	42	21	7	14	80	57	49
5	Dartford	42	18	8	14	75	58	48
6	Weymouth	42	21	5	16	69	43	47
7	Yeovil Town	42	18	11	13	67	51	47
8	Hillingdon Borough	42	20	6	16	64	58	46
9	Margate	42	19	8	15	74	68	46
10	Wimbledon	42	19	7	16	75	64	45
11	Romford	42	16	13	13	54	49	45
12	Guildford City	42	20	5	17	71	65	45
13	Telford Utd	42	18	7	17	83	68	43
14	Nuneaton Borough	42	16	10	16	46	47	42
15	Bedford Town	42	16	9	17	59	66	41
16	Worcester City	42	17	7	18	46	57	41
17	Cambridge City	42	12	14	16	68	71	38
18	Folkestone	42	14	7	21	57	64	35
19	**POOLE TOWN**	42	9	11	22	41	72	29
20	Bath City (R)	42	11	4	27	45	86	26
21	Merthyr Tydfil (R)	42	7	8	27	29	93	22
22	Gravesend & Northfleet (R)	42	5	6	31	30	110	16

POOLE TOWN F.C.

v

CHELMSFORD CITY

Southern League Premier Div.   Kick-off 3.0 p.m.

Saturday, 30th October, 1971

3p

LUCKY NUMBER   073

This Programme is Published by The Supporters' Club
Printed by The Ashley Press, Balena Close, Creekmoor Trading Estate, Poole. Tel. Broadstone 5656.

FOR REPORTS OF TODAY'S MATCHES AND CLUB NOTES READ TONIGHT'S... SPORTS ECHO *On sale at all Newsagents*

Chapter 13: Life After Football

Rod presenting a football to the golden gamble winner at the Watford match on 5/5/07 at the Madjeski Stadium

After Rod had retired from football, the family settled into life on the South Coast with frequent trips in the summer to Sandbanks beach and Poole Quay in the evenings where the kids were given a pack of crisps and a panda pop in the car while the adults would have a drink in the pub!

Rod continued working as a milkman and a French polisher, and there was an opportunity to meet up with his ex-teammate at Poole Town, Rod Taylor, who was running a junior team called Broadstone Bruins. Rod Taylor had been released by Poole Town the year before Rod and, throughout his career, had played for Portsmouth, Gillingham and Bournemouth, where he had played against Rod a few times.

Rod's eldest son, Stephen, had joined the Bruins playing centre back, so Rod would sometimes give Rod Taylor a hand with the coaching, particularly with some defence training. Together, they helped in guiding the Bruins to a cup final which they unfortunately lost.

As time went on, though, Rod became too busy with his French polishing and restoration business to help with the coaching and therefore had to stop helping out.

The only football Rod would play after he left Poole Town for Unigate in five-a-side matches at Poole Sports Centre in the mid-seventies.

Rod was asked to play in Jackie Fisher's testimonial match for Poole Town against a Southampton X1 in 1980 at the Poole Stadium for a midweek evening match. Rod turned up with his two sons, Stephen and Ian, to watch the game, and when Jackie knew Rod was there, he tried to twist Rod's arm to get him to play, but Rod declined as it had been too long since he had played.

It was in 1980 that Rod, Janet and family moved back to Berkshire after selling the house in West Way and put the money into a shared venture with his brother Alan, a farmer by trade, to purchase a smallholding in Barkham, near

Wokingham, called Edneys Hill Farm. Here, Rod and Janet ventured into the world of smallholding farmers keeping pigs and young cattle. Rod also built a workshop and continued as a French polisher and a furniture restorer, doing occasional work for ex Reading FC director Duncan Vincent.

Whilst working as a French polisher and furniture restorer, Rod would do some work for a few celebrities, namely Greg Lake of the group, Emerson, Lake and Palmer, Felix Bowness of Hi De Hi fame, Glen Hoddle, and his old manager Roy Bentley who was still living near Reading.

Rod also knew Maurice Evans well from his playing days and had stayed in contact with him. Maurice had offered Rod a scouting role while he was managing Oxford Utd in the mid-eighties, but Rod declined as he was happy with his work as a French polisher, and he didn't really have enough time to commit to helping Maurice out.

In 1982, Rod and Janet moved to Brook House in Barkham Street, another smallholding in partnership with his brother Alan. Unfortunately, Alan died not long after they had moved and after a lengthy court battle with Alan's family, Rod and Janet raised enough funds to purchase Brook House outright. Rod continued working as a French polisher.

In 2005, Rod and Janet moved to Finchampstead, and Rod started to wind down his French polishing business, finally retiring in 2015 and settling into retirement.

Rod was invited to the Madejski Stadium on 5th May 2007 for the home match against Watford in the Premiership to present a golden gamble winner with a signed football.

Reading lost the game 2-0. How they would have loved a Rodney Thornhill 4 goal haul in this match as this was the clubs first-ever season in the top division, and they missed out on the UEFA cup spot by just one point!

Rod still occasionally watches football on the TV and last went to see a live match in 2016 when he watched Hungerford v Poole Town with the author and friend, Stephen Rex. Rod's views on the game today are as follows:

"The game has changed a lot since I was playing. In the teams that play these days, the players seem to stroll about and build it up slowly, so the matches themselves can be quite boring. There is no urgency, and it's all about keeping the ball, whereas we used to want to get the ball up to the front men and support them and build it up quickly. Roy Bentley was a centre forward, and I think he wanted it up to the frontman quickly and play from there. The centre forward can hold it up, the other players can push up, and the play is quicker. Now they pass to the full-back, and he plays it back to the keeper; I find it a bit boring. I think it's a bit too tactical now.

When I played, the goalkeeper used to get the ball, go to the edge of his box, and get the ball halfway up the field. Now they knock it to the full-back who plays it to the winger, and he plays it inside and then it's played back again, and by that time, the opposing forwards are defending with their defence, so it's more difficult to do anything.

On the Reading side at the moment, I like the look of Lucas Joao upfront as he controls the ball, lays it off and then gets into a position to move up again, so they are starting to build up. I think he's quite good at it as he wins the ball all of the time in the air as he's so big, so if he's doing that, you are now in control of the game, as long as other players are moving off the ball.

I think the defenders these days tend to back off too much, and they let other teams come at them, which means the other team gets nearer the goal. If you hold them up a bit further up in midfield, they've got further to go to your goal, but these days they retreat to the edge of the box and let the other team shoot from there. It's just inviting pressure.

I like to see players looking around and seeing how the play is shaping up and making decisions from there, but I think these days, it's more about the shape you have to be in. If you are playing the ball about and moving about, I think it's more interesting, but it's just too slow these days and not as interesting.

I like the look of the Madejski Stadium, and the pitch looks nice and flat, and there is plenty of room, which is a bit different to some of the pitches I used to play on, particularly some of the northern team's pitches, which were more like park pitches!"

In early 2020, Rod was diagnosed with Alzheimer's disease, a disease prevalent in footballers who have spent a lot of time heading the ball. Rod is philosophical about it and acknowledges that his football playing days may have had a bearing on his Alzheimer's, but he doesn't regret his playing days one bit. His wife Janet was also diagnosed with Parkinson Disease many years ago, but both celebrated their Diamond Wedding anniversary on 15th April 2021, with a card from Her Majesty, The Queen.

Rod and Jan celebrate their Diamond Wedding Anniversary

At the time of writing in July 2021, Rod participates in a project run in collaboration between the PFA and the Sporting Memories Foundation charity. Sporting Memories offers practical support to older people living with dementia, depression, or loneliness.

He was introduced to the Foundation through Rachel Walden at the PFA, who coincidentally is the daughter of ex Poole Town teammate Rod Taylor.

The PFA Sporting Memories Club is for former professional players living with dementia and is supported by volunteers who are themselves, former players. The players come together for companionship and friendship and to re-live fond memories of football.

Rod was present for the first-ever online meeting with other ex-professionals from around the country and reminisced about his playing career and the first-ever matches he saw as a kid

Two PFA Sporting Memories Clubs have been running online during the Covid lockdown, with additional sessions being planned. It is expected that members will eventually be able to meet face-to-face.

Rod also attended the first-ever Dementia Café run by Reading FC at the Madejski Stadium in February 2020, just before the Covid virus put everyone into lockdown. He was surprised to see ex-teammate Fred Sharpe there on the day and had a good chat with him about their time at Reading.

Rod and ex-teammate Fred Sharpe talk about their playing days at the Dementia Café at The Madejski Stadium

There are now many Facebook groups looking back on past years at Reading FC, such as Reading FC Royals and Biscuits. One supporter, when asked out of all the players who had played for Reading, would they like to have a drink with, chose Rod out of all the legends that had played for the club, and it is good to see Rod's name included in a couple of supporters all-time Reading squad. It shows that Rod is still very well thought of by club supporters.

Mick Travers, who played for Reading with Rod, were sometimes rivals for a position on the left, remembers Rod as a frank and easy-going person. He describes Rod as an outstanding player, an excellent defender, and a perfect marker. He believes that, although Rod achieved a lot in his career, he was good enough to accomplish a lot more if the dice had fallen differently.

July 2021 - Rod catches up with ex-teammate at Reading, Mick Travers

William Stobie, one of the administrators of Reading FC Biscuits and Royals, who also played for Reading Schools with Rod, says that Rod was one of most underrated players to play for Reading and Rod was picked to take out the opponent's danger man and would always do a good job.

Roger Ware, a Reading Chronicle reporter who would travel with the team in the later 1960s, remembers that Rod was often the forgotten player in matches because his role was usually to keep an eye on the opposition star player. Roger always remembers the manager sticking up for Rod at after matches press conferences when people would say, "Didn't see much of Rod today," and the manager would reply, "Yes, but you didn't see much of their star player either, did you?"

Stephen Rex was a young supporter on his long journey supporting the club, and he remembers Rod playing when he first started watching Reading play. He remembers Rod being a bit of a terrier winning the ball and laying it off and one of two or three players who stood out in the team.

David Downs, former club historian and author of many books on Reading FC, remembers Rod. "The three games I remember most were the 6-2 win over Watford when Rod scored 4 goals, the FA Cup tie at Hendon when Rod scored twice, George Harris got the other one, and I caught one of Rod's shots as I was standing just behind the Hendon goal, and his goal against Sheffield Wednesday at Elm Park in the FA Cup. Wednesday won 3-2 with a last-minute goal scored by Jim McCalliog and went on to reach Wembley, where they lost 3-2 to Everton in the FA Cup Final.

Chris Reeves, the current Poole Town FC chairman, remembers Rod playing for Poole Town He says Rod was a great performer in the Poole colours and was virtually ever-present in both his seasons at Poole.

Rod has fond memories of his career as a professional footballer. He played in a time when the emphasis was on playing football and less about the money you could earn from the game. He felt privileged to play for the team he had supported as a young boy, and he would have played for the club for free.

Rod is one of those rare football players who started playing for the team he supported as a young boy and then rose through the ranks to make 221 appearances for the first team, including an 82-match successive run. He scored 23 goals, with the highlight of his career, scoring 4 goals in the first 29 minutes of a league match against Watford. He had other league clubs interested in signing him throughout his Reading career, but he never considered playing for anyone but his home team.

Reading are no longer nicknamed "The Biscuit Men". They are now nicknamed "The Royals" and are celebrating their 150th anniversary in the 2021-22 season. Throughout their history; there cannot be many players who can come close to Rod as being a true 'Loyal Royal."

The Author's Tribute To Rod On The Reading FC Kit 2021-22 Season Celebrating 150 Years.

Printed in Great Britain
by Amazon